Goodbye Abstinence
Hello Heart

an ex-pharisee approach to true love waits

John Hewitt

TATE PUBLISHING *& Enterprises*

Published by Tate Publishing & Enterprises, LLC
127 E. Trade Center Terrace | Mustang, Oklahoma 73064 USA
1.888.361.9473 | www.tatepublishing.com
Tate Publishing is committed to excellence in the publishing industry. The company reflects the philosophy established by the founders, based on Psalm 68:11,
"The Lord gave the word and great was the company of those who published it."

Book design copyright © 2008 by Tate Publishing, LLC. All rights reserved.

Cover design by Jacob Crissup
Interior design by Lynly D. Taylor

Published in the United States of America
ISBN: 978-1-60462-714-5
1. Biblical Studies-Abstinence-Courage   2. Current Event
08.02.25

To Willie Dennis Chapman Hewitt

My mother, who has lived her life with more heart than any person I have known.

Author's Note

Any and all statements reflecting wisdom and truth within this concept of Heart Life can be certain to have originated in the very heart of God. They have come to me through both life experiences of my own and the recorded lessons of countless fellow pilgrims on our common journey together. Some I have had the privilege to learn from and know personally–others have mentored me through their writings and teachings and I look forward to a day to express my thanks. God used Keith Miller in his *A Taste of New Wine* to teach me more about praying and just talking to my heavenly Father than all the prayer conferences I have attended. Malcolm Smith so touched my life with his teaching on God's heart toward me and how He, the Father, looks at us and values us; I've more than once had to pull off the road so I could see where I was supposed to be driving while listening to his work. They were assisted in this tutoring by Max Lucado in his *The Applause of Heaven* and other writings. John Eldridge in *Wild at Heart, Journey of Desire* and *The Sacred Romance* that simply put flesh and muscle on a skeleton of thoughts about the heart. And then the leadership team of Thrall, McNicol, and Lynch with *True Faced*–life as it can be without the masks. What an impact!

I am a pilgrim who is learning many of life's lessons by the "trial and error" curriculum–and am amazed that God would give me the privilege to put some of those lessons on paper and use them for good. These thoughts have been organized then in this present context by one who seeks with you, the Way, the Truth and the Life.

Thank you for joining me on this journey–John Hewitt

Table of Contents

Introduction

Dear Reader,

Welcome to what I hope may well be the ride of your life.

The message of this book will at times sound like I am talking to parents or youth pastors or an adult audience, especially if you, the reader, are in your teens. That is on purpose. One reason is because there is nothing about this that is kids stuff. Since you, regardless of your age, seem to be mature enough to be caring about how successful you are tackling this arena of relationships, or someone cares enough about you to have given you this book to read. Then hopefully you are also open to some thoughts and ideas, and the possibility that there just might be some more mature ways to attack life than "if it feels good, do it!" It must be the "Dad" part of me coming out to want to explain it to the other people in your world and those who have experienced life beyond your present age so they can be an encouragement to you and each other and also get a feel for where we are going with this. When you become the Mom or Dad in a few years, you are going to want to have a way to help your kiddos walk this journey for themselves. This concept of heart life is intended as an encouragement for readers of all ages. When I was a teenager, and then even as a young adult I thought anyone 10 years older than myself was "old". There was no way they still had the same desires and thoughts I did. That thought process was simply not true. None of us are without the possibility of finding ourselves, at any age–you heard it right younger set–at any age ... finding ourselves in circumstances and places where we wish, or we will wish tomorrow, we had handled the situation differently. Wishing perhaps to have made better choices of how we responded to an "opportunity" for intimacy with someone, maybe someone we work with or go to school with or live next door to, or maybe just met for the first time. The reason is both good news and bad news, depending on how you look at it.

The BAD NEWS is, the desires for romance and relational intimacy never go away.

The GOOD NEWS is, the desires for romance and relational intimacy never go away.

But how did this issue of passion come about in the first place? It had to start somewhere? It will help our process of working thru this material by saying, and remembering as we go along, that God does not view passion as a bad thing! Even romantic passion. It might also help if we went a step further and said He started it in the first place. If anybody is to blame—it's His fault! I (John) am glad He did, start it I mean. I personally kind of like it (that passion and romance and all that goes with it thing), a lot!

It will also be encouraging if we could also fully grasp the concept that God has placed within each of us a deep desire for intimacy–first in a relationship with Him and then with each other. *"Love the Lord your God with all your heart and with all your soul and with all your strength and with all your mind; and,* (or as a result of that first love with God)

Luke 10:27 (Editorial parenthesis mine).

Let's see where this goes…

One

A Better Way

"There has simply got to be a way!"

"A way to what?"

"Oh, you know, to help our kids listen to wisdom—to some good, sound advice about dating and sex and relationships–you know, just some good, think tank kind of stuff."

"You mean the good, sound advice and wisdom you wouldn't listen to at their age?"

"Okay then, oh wise one, what would you suggest we try? We have to do something!"

"I know you're right–but what do we do?"

"I hate to admit it but most of what I learned to expect from relationships was from my buddies–and locker room bragging."

"But the kids now are seeing so much more on TV and in movies … "

"And, on the internet—than we ever heard from anywhere."

"But they are not getting it right any better than we did– and maybe not even as well. So there must be a better way."

And I want to suggest there is!

Let's look at a couple of the options that are being pushed right now:

Option Number 1: Learn how to have Safe Sex (whatever that is)—and you will most likely learn how to let your emotions call the shots in your life. And, you'll probably learn to feel confident playing close to the fire. My suggestion with this approach is that you had better hope and pray that by chance, or by being smart enough (like that is going to happen), that you won't get burned. I do, however, wish you well in the Safe Sex approach. You're actually going to need it! You do have the "help" of some educational and government programs and a large portion of our society joining with you in this concept and many, many options from which to choose. Good luck!

Option Number 2: Ah, then maybe learning to Just Say No to romance and sex is a better plan. As we will see later on, there are times when No is not just one of the possible answers, it can be the best answer for a particular situation. And, if you can live a disciplined life and make the tough decisions at the right time, the Just Say No approach may work well for you. Some people are able to. It didn't work very well for me. Oh, I wanted it to work, for sure. But the need for being liked, even desired, and the validation I thought would come through the response of others was way too warm and tasty for me to be willing to live on the dry toast of abstinence alone.

Either of these two plans does offer the side benefits of possibly helping protect you from STD's (Sexually Transmitted Diseases), and from having babies before you are married, and may even save your family and your church (if you are involved in one) from huge disappointment and pain. But then, maybe not.

I'm thinking there is still yet another and, I suggest, better way to flesh out (no pun intended) this dating and romance and sex thing.

But before we go very far, I want you to realize that this approach to relationships is not safe. But the truth is, it is not "safe", at least not from the standpoint that it cannot be misused. That simply means that the ideas and concepts for life that we are about to look at together are not a guaranteed "you won't have any problems in your life if you do this" process. In fact the information and thought processes you are about to be encouraged to enter into can be incredibly helpful, or they could be used selfishly to manipulate others to achieve your own little personal "me" agenda. The reason I say this concept is not safe is because anything that has a potential for good, also has by its very nature an equal potential for harm. A drug can be used for medicinal purposes, for instance, and can be incredibly helpful and meet many needs in a really good way, or it can be very harmful if used wrongly or taken the wrong way. A really great example of something that can be used wisely or unwisely is a computer. A computer, in and of itself is neither good or bad. Its ability to process and store data at high speeds makes it a remarkable tool for scientific research, business, and education. The capability of a computer to access the internet, has an incredible potential for good with its ability to communicate and transfer information almost anywhere in the world. This capability, however, makes this same computer a tool capable of great misuse with what can be communicated. And, a computer's ability to process data and transfer information is some of the very avenues by which hackers and identity theft operators ply their trades.

So is the information in this book safe in and of itself? No Way! It is good, and it can be incredibly helpful! But it is not safe.

But neither are romance and desire and intimacy and all that can be associated with them safe either. It wouldn't be all it was created to be if you could pre-program our moods and desires, or set them up through a timer or something to come on and go off at certain situations. It's not like your coffee maker that comes on at 6:00 a.m. and goes off automatically after two hours so it won't burn the house down. When we talk about romance, we are talking about a biological, emotional, hormone powered, percolator that can come on, at some of the seemingly most inopportune times and can quickly exceed the boiling point–and will burn the house down if left unattended! That is a part of what makes it what it is. And you and I actually wouldn't want it any other way.

So what do we do with this "unsafe" thing we call intimacy and romance and desire? Can we learn a path to live with it? I sure believe so. Can we really *live* without it? Don't even want to try?

Moms and dads have already been attempting to do something with it for a long time, you know. Your parent's parents assuredly did, your folks tried, you probably are working on it, and even your children (when you have some) most likely will, attempt to learn for themselves and then teach their children that there are "right ways" and "wrong ways" to explore life. And it didn't just start with the last three or four generations of parents and kids. The very first parent ever (God) set out guidelines of how things could be and should be, and He knew full well the risk of allowing those first "kids" the freedom of making choices for themselves. (Just an early note of encouragement for the moms and dads reading with us: Even the best parent ever had disobedient kids! And in the same vane of thought for you the pilgrim on this journey with me, the kids with the best parent ever–made unwise choices! Now there is a group I can hang with.)

And when you think back on it, most of what has been discussed with you, or is currently being discussed by your parents and anyone who cares about you, focuses on what *not* to do, who to *stay away* from, and where *not to go.* And if you would ask them, most of what they were told by their parents was the same thing. The problem seems to come in the fact that there simply are not enough *no's, stay away from's,* and *don't go there's* to cover every situation that life can throw at you. So the list has to keep expanding to keep up with the options that are out there, sometimes not fast enough.

What you want for your life, what I want for my life, and I'll bet what your folks want for you too, is this: To navigate thru life well. To make wise decisions about:

Relationships
Boy friends
Girl friends
Activities
Career paths
Life partners
Everything!

To really make those choices well it will help–no, it is important–actually, it is **huge** to understand who you are, as an individual. Who *you* really are. The stripped bare, naked, gut level—*you*. I'm not talking about when you are all dolled up with a new hair do and your favorite outfit on or your name brand shorts or shirt. I'm not even referring to you in your new car or your latest achievements in band or sports or academics. I'm talking about the you that looks in the mirror when you first get up in the morning and stumble into the bath room in the morning *before* you "fix" anything. The you whose breath stinks, and needs to pee, and whose face and hair look like God alone knows what. That you! I'm most certainly *not* talking about the *you* based on who somebody else says you are, or should be, especially by their responses to you. So, in addition to looking at how we relate to other people, a part of this process is going to be taking a look at who we are as an individual and what we have to offer to someone else. Maybe even why would we offer ourselves, and in what ways might we offer ourselves to others. (It might sound like heavy "think tank" kind of stuff, but it is really fun to see a little of *why* we do what we do. Sometimes it is not only fun to see the thoughts behind the action, it can be pretty funny as well. And when it is funny, we'll laugh with each other together.)

Like it or not we are relational to the core. There are very few, if any, true loners out there. We simply are not wired that way. You want some buddies or someone to hang out with and so do I. At times it seems it would be simpler if we could go it alone, if we didn't need anybody. How much simpler could that be? I don't have to put up with you and you don't have to tolerate me and…you know what I mean. Some of us actually try to prove we don't need anybody else, but it usually creates more problems than solutions because we were created for relationships. Remember Adam (the only guy ever without a belly button) in the biblical account of creation? He was in the Garden of Eden all by himself except for his buddies in the animal kingdom. So if being a loner was intended to be the best plan, Adam had it made. There was no one borrowing and not returning his stuff (whatever "stuff" he had). No one made noise and woke him up when he was trying to sleep. No one even ate the last piece of pie that he had been saving just for the right time. It was just Adam, and God. But here is where God says the first recorded *"It is not good… " (Gen 2:18).* Everything that has gone on in creation before this time, God has said repeatedly, "It is good." The stars, the seas and dry land, the birds, the fish and all plants (even poison ivy?), all animal life, God has said, "It is good." The rest of that verse says, though, what was not good. "It was not good … *for man to be alone."* Why? Because he (Adam), me, we, you, need help. We need each other. We need relationships and we do best when we live in community with others. So He, God, creates Eve. Now ladies, you are not the problem, but you being here on planet earth with us guys sure seems to help identify that there is one. Anyway, as we are relational at the depths of who we are, it should be no surprise that being accepted and liked is major to all of us. Watch how this plays out. When we begin to grow up and desire to be out from under our parents "wings" of authority and begin to become independent as individuals, we will want to test our "own" wings. We want to expand our world beyond just our immediate own family, and we find ourselves desperate for someone to acknowledge us by their acceptance, usually our friends, or wish they were my friends, for those "if you like me I must be okay" responses. In fact at this "growing independent" time in life, one of our greatest fears is being alone, "invisible", left out. We're going to discuss why this is so important in a little bit, but for now understand this fear of being left out, or alone, can give a lot of power to "the group" over the individual in the often unspoken law, "we will exclude you if you don't fit in with the established expectations", whatever they are. You know exactly what I am talking about. Just knowing this fact doesn't take away the pressure of trying to be accepted, but it can help to realize that a lot of what motivates us in the way we act toward others, whether with confidence–because we already know we are accepted, or with timidity, because we aren't sure where we stand just yet, is actually the influence of the group on us.

You may disagree and feel that being liked and accepted is no big deal to you. You can take it or leave it, right? You don't need anyone's approval. Then don't pitch a fit the next time your "in" jeans or favorite shirt or top aren't clean and ready to wear when you need them. Go on and put on that *other* stuff in your closet that you don't feel it is "really" your style or up to your standards. Maybe something your Mom or Grandma bought you on sale at the "wrong store" and go out in confidence. Oh, and be sure and don't offer any excuses to you friends for your outfit when asked later in the evening what you were thinking when you dressed like that. You don't care what other people think, so why would you even offer to explain that you do have the "good stuff", it's just at home? Or, the next time you and the guys are choosing sides for a game of ball, choose first the guy who can't dribble **or** shoot, and genuinely treat him like you are glad he came to play. Treat him like he is more important than the final score (like the score will really matter six months from now). Be willing to take the heat from the other team members with their looks and stares as the game progresses. No big deal, right? Careful, you'll set off the smoke alarm!

There is good news though, when it comes to the influence or to this "group power" thing. It can also work in your favor if the particular group you want to run with has some good character qualities and actually encourages good decisions and activities. Don't down play the incredible influence we have on each other, especially in group settings. It can be very significant.

Somewhere along the way one of the biggest measuring sticks for checking out how well we are doing in being accepted relationally, at this independent stage in life, seems to be how "beautiful and desirable" one might be. Are we "hot", what do others say about us, are we popular, and why? Which seems to be typically evaluated by how we are pursued and responded to by each other physically–yes, even sexually. The TV and movie world has not helped any in this mindset either. It looks and feels so "adulty", so grown up to be physical or get some level of physical response from someone. How many times have you heard the line played out in a movie or book "Did he kiss you?" being the first question for a girl to ask her sister or roommate when she comes in from a first date with "Mr. Studly". Like that is the standard that signals that you have got it going on, Babe, you are truly something irresistible. I mean if I think "she" is the princess, and she thinks I'm sharp, then just maybe, I am the prince! Believe it or not, romance and sex are not anywhere near all there is to being relational, but in the teens and even many years later into life this is not nearly so clear. This hazy area of physical response, and how much response—yes or no to what–can create a real potential battle for all of us, especially as young adults and even younger teens to confidently know where to stand when the pressure of the group or an individual seems to call for pushing against the boundaries of both your parents' guidelines and what you may personally even feel comfortable with when it comes to how to relate with each other.

Okay, then it sounds like the simple way is to go right back with the "Just Say No" concept of romance.

Maybe yes, maybe not necessarily so.

Remember, I shared earlier that the disciplined approach of just saying no didn't work very well for me. Let me share why I think it didn't. How about because there are just times when *No* is almost impossible to say. Saying No to the warm passionate invitation of someone you really want to be liked and accepted by is more than tough. Saying No to the constant invitations of a friend or a "'wish you were my friend" relationship to: have a beer, try a smoke, take a dip "for your lip", it feels like you are going against everything that is within you. It seems like guaranteed relational death, and who knows what else. Everybody else is doing it, right? Whatever *it* is, or I think they are. And remember, at this "time to relocate the boundaries" age in my life, I *do not* want to stand out too much, or I could risk being left out completely.

The ineffectiveness of a just say no approach is why a wise parent tells their child to stay off of lover's lane or out of their girlfriend/ boyfriend's house when there aren't any parents at home. They know, *from experience*, that it is a heck of a lot easier to make a good decision where to go or be "place wise"— *before* you go there, than it is to be there, coupled up, and then try to say no to the guy or gal on the couch or the car seat next to you who may be wanting things to go in a more touchy, feely, responsive direction.

The main reason "no"

ADDED ATTRACTION

You want an interesting conversation with your folks sometime? Ask them how they got so much experience and wisdom to know it is not a good idea to get in a hot romantic situation—and then try to say no.

doesn't work very well long term is, No simply doesn't have the power that Yes has! You try it. There is a huge energy dynamic difference in saying *yes* to good eating habits and exercise, for example, as a choice for a healthy life style versus hoping to stay trim and fit by always saying *no* to every wonderful, gooey, amazing, scrumptious, incredibly delicious ... (sorry, I almost lost it there) ... treat the world has to offer. You know it is true. Saying Yes to something, especially something that is right and good and honorable carries a lot more weightiness with the decision than it's negative counterpart can offer.

Saying *no* to something, even a possible wrong something, requires an act of resolve or discipline—perhaps even fear. And how many times will you say no to something that is really desirable and tempting to you? (If you didn't feel you really wanted it or needed it, it wouldn't be such a temptation to try!) At some point your emotions will override your logic and say, "you owe this to yourself"–or "this isn't such a big deal." When you say *no* to something, especially something so alluring and desirable as physical response, you get this feeling inside that you are giving up something big and really missing out, or that you are ruining this relationship you wanted so much to work. And keep in mind that every fiber in your own physical emotional and nervous system may not be helping very much by yelling to you that you really do *want this* in the first place.

The real question is–want what?

Because you do!

What?

Want that.

That what?

Now we're getting somewhere!

G. K. Chesterton said, "When a man knocks on the door of a brothel, he is really looking for God." I believe he is right, and I think before we're through you'll see why and possibly even agree. (You hoped I was going to tell you what a brothel is? Come on work with me here a little bit. If you don't know that term, look it up!)

One of the keys, if not the key to great romance and great passion and keeping it all in a right perspective is to understand what we really are looking for. We need a way to help see the heart *behind* our desires. We'll go into further detail in later sessions, but for now recognize, and hopefully agree with me, that *we were* made for love and passion and to live life with desire. Believe it or not, we were made to live in relationship with our Creator. His is the great heart of love, the one who refers to Himself as the bridegroom and we his bride. He is the one who pursues *us* with passion, and is jealous for us when we act like prostitutes toward smaller loves than His. He wants to invite us back into His larger story—that is why He came to redeem us. In Luke 10:27 He says, *"Love the Lord your God with all your heart and with all your soul and with all your strength and with all your mind'; and,* (or as a result of that first love with God) *'Love your neighbor as yourself."* (Editorial parenthesis mine). He did not come and go thru the path of crucifixion so that we could hopefully be good and play nice with each other. He didn't even come so that we could do a better job of keeping the rules—and "just saying no" to the bad stuff. Imagine that!

Let me take a time out.

I need to say that I realize not everyone who reads this book is going to have the same concept of God that I express in these pages, or beliefs, or even perceived need for a relationship with God. Nor are we all likely to agree on what role He plays—or doesn't play in life. In the context of this material, I'm okay with that. I for one, however, cannot address the concepts of love and romance and intimacy from any other direction than what I genuinely believe to be true.

Okay, Time in.

The rules have always been there, guidelines and principles for life to help us make good choices and to expose us when we don't follow them and to help us see who we are. To remind us we would never get life right enough on our own. He, Jesus, came to bring us back to life, to restore fellowship, us with God. To bring our hearts back to life.

"For the wages of sin is death but the gift of God
in Christ Jesus is eternal life" (Romans 6:23).

"Yet to all who believed him, to those who believed in his name,
he gave the right to become children of God" (John 1:12).

I hope you know, and I want you to understand that I know that this book is not *the answer*. It is a tool. Hopefully a good tool that you the reader can use, whether you are 13 or 73, whether you are a parent, a youth pastor, or a teacher. That you younger guys and gals, and adults, can work through in a small study group setting or even on your own and be encouraged about who you are, and how this arena of relationships and interaction with each other fits rightly as a part of that much bigger story that was going on before you or I were even born.

This need for validation and response and the myriad of ways we attempt seeking to find our value is so strong that it is amazing. The created desire that is within us for intimacy—yes even physical intimacy is like hot coals that burn inside of us. If all you give me to control it with is a set of rules—even rules that may sound right, and have good intentions, but you give me no power to carry them through, I am toast! Just because you show me the sign on the side of the highway that tells me the speed limit, in no way gives me the desire, or the power to keep the law. The highway patrolman parked on the side of the road might make me want to follow the speed guidelines (the rules and potential consequences approach). Cows that have gotten out of their fenced pastures and are feeding along the roadside might (risk of danger from ignoring the rules). Children playing in the yards and chasing balls into the street might (my being thoughtful of the risk to others of my actions). The motivation to be a good citizen might (doing something simply because it is a right thing to do). Not the sign!

This desire for response, for validation, for love, is in all of us; and is a fire that will demand attention. "Either kill me or feed me," it says, "but you will not be successful in ignoring me. It will cost you something to attempt to lock me away with rules and guidelines—and it will cost you something to let me run free, unchecked and consuming."

I understand disciplines and systems with rules and guidelines. I'm an engineer by education and an organizer by personality. Disciplines and systems have a place and a purpose. That's the way engineers think and do things. But there is nothing so tasteless and undesirable as a person, or group of people who have no passion in their lives, or for life itself who live their lives by disciplines alone, even great disciplines. In 1 Peter 3:15 scripture says, *"Always be prepared to give an answer to everyone who asks you to give the reason for the hope that you have."* Allow me to ask you the same question that caught me up short when I was asked, "When was the last time someone noticed enough hope in your life to ask about it?" When was the last time there was enough difference about your life that anyone would notice? Me either. ("Welcome to the lost in the crowd club. Let me show you around, I've been a member for a long time.")

So there must be a way to get beyond this hurdle of testing the waters, physically and relationally, that does not require faking what is true about us as humans with our passions and desires, but at the same time doesn't destroy us.

You may be a person whose conscience may not let you go but "so far" in physical response. Maybe you won't go "as far as" some of your buddies or perhaps you would "never do what you see in movies." Be careful, if you are naïve about this you will, sometimes without even realizing it, find yourself having created your own personal and private ways to "warm" by the fire. It can be as subtle as an obsession with romance novels (yes, even Christian romance novels), movies and television. Not reading for fun or enjoying a good book, but actually losing one's self into someone else's intimate story. You know exactly what I'm talking about. If you personally haven't done so, you have friends who would not even *think* about missing an episode of some TV series where the actors are "soooo" hot and the romances are too. Like, "I'll just die if Justin doesn't marry Camden!" Now that's really big, ho hum.

Guys, I think we are more into this next area than the ladies because we are much more visual in our appetites and in the ways we get turned on. The internet and all that is available there can capture us in ways you may not have imagined. Some of you know exactly what I mean. Anyway, we'll talk in more detail in the guy's section.

Others of us develop the "I know I can stop at whatever place I want to" mentality. We learn how to "play" with romance and sex, but hopefully not go too far. Be careful! Your heart is more involved here than you realize. Some of these "less dangerous" ways can often lead to other more "limited paths" of sexual expression, paths that are again, at least "not as bad as", with the thought that no one can get hurt by this, or this isn't really sex is it? Perhaps heavy petting or oral sex or masturbation—you can't get pregnant doing that can you?

Just a brief word of caution while we are here: All of these ways of managing ourselves in how we physically respond to one another can develop mental habits and very possibly stimulant patterns that can follow you into adulthood and believe it or not, can affect your ability to give yourself confidently and fully to the physical relationship portion in even a great marriage later in life.

In an interaction time with some teens from the youth group at our church, the question was very bravely posed, "Do you lose your virginity by having oral sex?" Another student asked, "At what point do you actually lose your virginity?" These were great questions that set us all as sponsors back a little on our "comfort zones", but they were questions that represented the deep desire to put some manageable handles on this issue of sex. The real question being asked was, "How close can I get and not cross the line of too far?"

A friend of mine mentioned a phone call he received from a dad who was broken-hearted over his 17 year-old daughter when he found out she was pregnant. The dad said, "And she has been through three True Love Waits conferences, how could this happen?"

What if—

> What if–*you could begin to understand* that the very deepest desires of your heart for intimacy and validation are God-given and they are good and have a purpose and fit rightly in His plan for your life?

"I will give you a new heart and put a new spirit in you; I will remove from you your heart of stone and give you a heart of flesh. And I will put my Spirit in you and move you to follow my decrees and be careful to keep my laws" (Ezekiel 36: 26–27).

What if–*you could recognize* when you are seeking answers and validation from sources and in ways that *cannot* give you value or answers?

What if—*you begin to see* the deep needs that you are attempting so desperately to meet such as the desire for physical and emotional intimacy (which society often lumps together and calls it sex) and see you just may be asking the wrong sources.

What if–*you allow room* for your Abba Father to reveal His heart toward you and see the deepest desires of your heart as good, a gift for your life now and a beacon of hope for a future yet to come?

Do we *dare admit together*, that there still *is* a path to the tree of the knowledge of good and evil? A place where life changing choices are made, and realize if you enjoy its fruit (in an out of intended design context), it still will bring pain and assuredly death even as in the garden of old? You know the tree is there. You see and hear your friends talk about the rush of response and sense there is something "grown up" about this activity of life.

What if–do we dare? Do we dare not?

At the time of this writing, our two daughters, Katie and Rebekah, are in their late teens and early twenties; I'm thinking pretty hard on this one right now.

How long and how much can I dictate their decisions?

Do I really want to?

Is that what is best for them, Mom and Dad calling the shots—not a totally bad plan, at least from *my* (the dad's) perspective. I always thought "arranged" marriages were the most ridiculous thing I had ever heard of, until I became a father of girls. Now at times I think I can see some real plusses to the concept. (My daughters still cringe at the thought–though I can't imagine why.)

What options do I have available with which to really influence them?

How much do I have a say about what they accept as "theirs" for their lives?

How do we help them find their own way? Ultimately they have to decide for themselves. Every person gives an answer for his/her own life both to themselves and to their Creator.

Job 31:14, "what will I do when God confronts **me**? What will I answer when called to account?" (bold type mine)

Romans 14:12, "So then, each of us will give an account of himself to God."

Before there were *any* permanent women in my own life, I had the opportunity to work with a Young Life group of high school kids. I saw some incredible young men and women. They came from good homes and they sure seemed to "have their heads on straight". A few years later, I was naively surprised to run into some of these same kids in some very different settings. Places where I would have never expected to find them based on what they said and seemed to imply a few years earlier. (Okay, what was I doing there to run into them? I'm still a work in process too, you know. That's why I turned in my Pharisee card, remember?)

Anyway, I believe God showed me that great homes can have great kids, and as long as the kids are at home, Mom and Dad's rules and guidelines seem to work fine and most kids walk along well between these protective fences. But when you go off to college or move out into the working world, Mom and Dad's rules can become very inconvenient and restricting and don't seem to apply. (My parent's rules sure did–become inconvenient.) So, we test the waters, under the "helpful" guidance and influence of our friends, and begin to decide what we are going to believe and accept for ourselves and base our lives upon.

And if you haven't already, you will too. Come to that place when you will begin to decide what standards you are going to live your life upon. You cannot live out someone else's convictions, even if those convictions are very good. At some point you have to own them. The beliefs for your life have to become yours. It is a wise parent (what I refer to as coaches for life) that can help us see that the rules and guidelines applied at home, and maybe at church, are not theirs, but God's (which the good one's are), and that they are for our good, and for our protection and that these guidelines are right (because they are). God doesn't say something to make it right, the things God says are right.

The law of the Lord is perfect reviving the soul.
The statutes of the Lord are trustworthy making wise the simple.
The precepts of the Lord are right giving joy to the heart.
The commands of the Lord are radiant, giving light to the eyes.
Psalms 19: 7–8

That God's concepts and guidelines apply in our world every day and go with us no matter who we are or where life may take us.

Jeremiah 23:23–24 tells us, "Am I only a God nearby, and not a God far away? ... Can anyone hide in secret places so that I cannot find him?"

Let me throw in a concept of looking at scripture that you may not have made room for before. What if the "guide-lines, and yes, even the commandments, and the rules" are not just guidelines, and commandments, and rules? What if the designer of life has actually given us more than "take the fun out of everything" commands and offered to us concepts and principles for living. Who would know better how to navigate through life well than the very designer of that life? What if these concepts and principles, if followed, would actually make your life, and my life come out better than if we violated these same concepts and principles?

I realize if we open the door for this view we may also have to make room for the possibility that some of the struggles and discipline and correction that impacts our lives is actually for our good, not just slamming us for doing wrong. Don't buy into this at full speed yet, just allow for the possibility.

But if that has any merit, then with His help, we may just be successful in formulating a concept for life and a belief structure that is really ours and that can weather the questions life will ask of you now, and in the future. And maybe, just maybe, you will know where you stand on the important stuff and why you make the choices you make, and we will not depart from that which is right and good, and which we have begun to embrace as our own.

The purpose of this approach in safeguarding our relationships, then, is to recognize the invitation God is giving us to live in the larger story of His redemption and to live life from our hearts–from our deep hearts, with passion and desire and a sense of the adventure and fellowship for which He has redeemed us.

It merits repeating, Jesus Christ did not die on a cross so we might be good boys and girls, so that we might be nice, or even sexually pure. He died to set us free to be the bride we were created to be in the first place, and to live in an affair of love with Him. One that will require our whole heart, and the total purposed will of our mind and of our soul.

" ... Love the Lord your God with all your heart and with all your soul and with all your strength and with all your mind; and, Love your neighbor as yourself." (Luke 10:27).

Two

Life Concepts–
The Bottom Line

If you have been a teenager for more than thirty minutes, you have heard talks or been encouraged to read materials on or been instructed by your parents about whom to date, how to date, when to date, where to go or not go if you date, and what not to do on a date or in a relationship. At school you have probably heard from your friends or even in a class setting how to "do it" and not get burned–how to have "safe sex". So why this book, or why one more attempt at this thing we refer to as romance and relationships and even sex? One would think pretty much all of the bases have been covered by now. As the title of this book implies, we are going to set aside some of the more familiar paths and look at this world of desire and response from a different angle than the typical approach. We are going to confess up front again that relationships and romance with the desire for intimacy and all that can be packaged together with that are not only a big part of life, but also a very powerful part of something that is good. It bears repeating and to keep repeating–passion and desire and intimacy are not bad things, *they are good!*

We also said in Chapter One that so we can better keep both the whole issue of sex and romance in perspective to the larger story we are going to let the blame fall where it should—on God. He started this whole passion and desire thing in the first place. He made us with the attractions that arouse our appetites and can capture our minds. Also, remember the direction this approach is taking us. We are not just into the do's and don'ts, we are looking into the issues of the heart rather than just another set of rules and guidelines to try to keep. As I mentioned in the title to this whole adventure, I turned in my Pharisee (religious rule keeper person types) card because I got tired of failing. Trying to live by rules that I didn't understand, or like, seldom agreed with, for the life of me couldn't keep, and that often didn't seem to even make sense for the situations I found myself in. I needed a better reason and understanding, or something. I needed a better way than "just saying no".

To tackle this area of relationships and intimacy we are going to start by laying down a base line, fundamental truths that all of our concepts will be based upon. These truths, or *Life Concepts* as we will call them, are not all there are as possibilities, but they are three basic and very critical and foundational principles for life:

LIFE CONCEPT No. 1

I LIVE MY LIFE BASED ON THE THINGS I BELIEVE TO BE TRUE.

And I do that whether they are actually true or not!

"For as He thinks within himself, so He is" (Proverbs 23:7 NAS).

LIFE CONCEPT No. 2

THE THINGS I BELIEVE ABOUT GOD—
DO NOT CHANGE THE TRUTH ABOUT
GOD AT ALL!

PS—neither does what anyone else
believes about God change the truth
about Him either.
(Not your friends, or your teachers,
or your pastor, or in all respect,
your parents.)

LIFE CONCEPT No. 3

ALL OF THE CRUCIAL ISSUES OF LIFE
COME FROM THE HEART—
guard it above all else.

*Proverbs 4:23 says, "above all else
guard your heart for it is
the wellspring of life."*

We are going to have some incredible discussions (some that may surprise you a little in where we go with this) and tackle and really chew on some of the deep questions we all have asked, or would like to.

Some of these issues are pretty personal and you may want to "think tank" through them alone before sharing your thoughts with a close friend. Others can be and will be approached very well, if desired, in a small group setting where you can benefit from each other's input. The group doesn't have to be very large to be really helpful—but the number one desired character quality for anyone you discuss this with is you want people who are trustworthy (this is not Chatty Kathy stuff). I have also found it important that the members of a small group be genuine seekers of truth. Not a bunch of air heads just looking for something to giggle about or somewhere to hang out one night a week, or whatever. Every discussion doesn't have to be and really should not be all serious or heavy—at times it is really kind of funny how badly we want a response from someone and the dumb things we will do trying to get it. Go with that. Let your heart laugh at our silliness.

There will also be occasion when you will be encouraged to spend time alone with God to seek His answer for your life. Some of you may have never spent time there or feel you would even know how. We'll work on it together. I have found it to be well worth the time you spend and the commitment you make to work through these issues. This is not a speed-reading course to see who can get to the end first. This is an opportunity for you to think tank a little and perhaps get to know yourself at a deeper level. And, allow God to show you what may prove to be a whole new approach to life.

On issues such as:

I.   What is true intimacy?

a.   Will there be anything like sex in heaven? (That one will get your Sunday School teacher's attention!)

b.   God, what did you have in mind here when you placed this desire within me? Why is it so alluring, so intriguing to share "closeness" with each other?

c.   What do I mean when I see an attractive person and my thoughts shout, "Whoa!" before I even realize my mind is in gear? Do I want her/him? Why or why not? Or, do I want that? That what?

    d.   So what has changed in our society? Did the guys get more testosterone or what? Or have we really changed so much from times in the past?

II.   What does it make me feel to be physically and emotionally close to someone and feel accepted by them? Who is them, anyway?

    a.   How close is too close? Can some people get "closer" than others without getting in trouble?

    b.   Is it okay for Christian couples to make out? How far should Christians go, physically, in their dating interactions? Is it different for Christians than those not professing a belief structure? Why and how is it different?

    c.   At what point do you lose your virginity? Are the standards the same for Christians and non-believers?

III.   "What is the big deal about magazines with nude pictures and internet sex sites. It doesn't affect me, I laugh at it. I can watch it and feel nothing."

IV.   How important is this heart issue to God anyway? Life Concept No. 3 says it is very big! Why?

V.   Is having babies and filling the earth a factor here? Didn't God say in Gen. 1:28 ... "Be fruitful and increase in number, fill the earth and subdue it"? If God made it feel as good as it seems like it would, how can it be so bad?

    a.   Isn't "abstinence" and "true love waits" really kind of outdated religious churchy stuff; because none of my friends at school or work really feel this way?

b. What do you mean when you talk about a "larger story"?

VI. What about the couples thing?

a. I know this isn't necessarily about abstinence or sex, but in many ways it is about the same spirit of relationships and their impact on each other.

b. How does it affect your youth group or your fellowship of friends when couples begin to form and date within the group? Is it no big deal–does it separate the fellowship of the group–does it even matter at all?

Three

The Larger Story–
Putting Things in Perspective

It is very important early on that we put this whole arena of relationships and physical response, and sex, in the context of the much larger picture; because there is a larger picture (story) going on. Romance and physical exploration is a part–and a significant part for sure, but only a part. It is not, as we can tend to think, the whole story. If you think of it in terms of the whole story, it will get way out of proportion and can dominate your thoughts and actions for a significantly long period of your life.

Remember,

> ## LIFE CONCEPT No. 1
>
> I LIVE MY LIFE BASED ON THE THINGS I BELIEVE TO BE TRUE.
>
> And I do that whether they are actually true or not!
>
> *"For as He thinks within himself, so He is"* (Proverbs 23:7 NAS).

If you believe response and relationships, and specifically sex, are the number one agenda for your life, you will act and live that way—and that will be a mistake.

It will help us to get our life in perspective to that larger story. That is to realize that there was something going on long before there were any of us on the scene. Before you were born, there was a story. What do I mean by that? Well, were you the one that dropped the apples so your pal Isaac Newton could measure gravity? Or hang out with Napoleon at Waterloo or help tie the string onto the kite with Ben Franklin to see if lighting was the "key" to electrical power? Better yet, read all the "begats" in Genesis from Chapter 5 on, or the record of the generations in the Book of Numbers, and even the first chapter of Matthew and see if any of those people were in your class at school. There have been people living and dealing with life for a very long time. Now it is coming up your turn.

Here is a thought to chew on: Do you fully realize that if your grandparents had never had any children—you probably wouldn't either? (Work with me here a little bit.)

I realize I am being silly here, but just pause and appreciate that many, many lives have come and lived and are now gone. All of those lives were once young, as you probably are, and had dreams of accomplishments and fears of failure. And they all experienced some of both as life unfolds, just like you and I do. Before your parents or grand parents were born, there was a story going on. Even before there was time, there was a story. And that story is part of a plan. And we need to remember that this story, God's plan, will be going on after you and I are gone. We were not the beginning of that story nor can we bring the story to a close. We were not responsible for thinking it up nor are we responsible for keeping it going. So, thankfully, we are not likely to be the ones that will bring it to its end. It is bigger than us, and that is good news. We were created to be a part and have been invited to *enter into* this larger story, and have even been offered a significant role that is ours to play–but we must enter in. (Put that thought of a "significant role that is ours to play" on the back burner for now, but we are going to come back and chew on it later.)

If we can keep the right perspective on where we fit and the parts we play, it will help relieve some of the pressure in a lot of areas and allow individual events and stages of growth in our lives to take their proper weightiness in this larger story. It might also add an interesting angle to the plot if we understand that the story we are living in was begun in love and that it was good. That from before the very beginning there was a bride-groom and there was a plan for a bride. And, that there was, and is, a villain who more than anything wants to destroy that story of love. (Add this information to that significant part to play thought mentioned in the last paragraph.)

Then relationships, yes, even relationships that are phys-ical in their context, and sex, are a part of *God's good plan.* In fact you may not remember but the first math homework assignment ever was given by God in Genesis 1:28 when He tells Adam and Eve "*to be fruitful and multiply*" [NAS] (lame, I know, I just couldn't pass up the opportunity.)

Enter stage left, you and I, and everybody else, looking for a way to satisfy our needs and wants for relational closeness. Bringing with us the belief that when it comes to dating, and sex … if so many people are doing it, everybody can't be wrong can they? There you go …

If I believe everybody is doing it (and to some degree I don't even care what **it** is). I mean, they can't all be wrong, can they? Then I'm going to be more likely to not want to be left out and be willing to give it a try myself. I'm going to begin to think and believe the rules and guidelines surely don't apply like I've been told. Somebody must be reading scripture wrong or that it's just so outdated that you can't go by that stuff anymore.

Well, let's see, there was...

"The earth is flat Columbus, you go too far and you'll fall off."

"Come on Wilbur (Wright), you can't fly. If man was meant to fly, God would have made him with wings."

"Roger (Banister), if a man ever tried to run a mile in less than 4 minutes, why his heart would burst"!

Then of course there was Noah vs. the whole earth. "It ain't gonna rain, Man, that boat is a waste of your time."

Jesus vs. established religion.

Joshua and Caleb vs. the rest of the tribe of Israel, and many, many more.

So you tell me, does the size of the crowd or the number of followers a concept has make something right? You know it doesn't! Check this advice out. Colossians 2:8 cautions us, "See to it that no one takes you captive through hollow and deceptive philosophy which depends on human tradition and the basic principles of this world rather than Christ."

Let's take a moment to look at a quick concept of thought...

The Think Tank Process

When a person is born again in Jesus Christ, (when someone has accepted the offer that Jesus makes that His life and His death could pay the price that God's law demands for our sins), God changes us at the level of the heart. 2 Corinthians 5:17, "Therefore, if anyone is in Christ, he is a new creation; the old has gone, the new has come!" As a result of that "newness", we can begin to think different (operative words here are "can begin"). In fact you begin to reason upside down or backwards, actually it is more inside out from the way you processed things before. Animals live by instinct, plants exist by God-established laws of nature, you and I live by choice. Everything God created, He called good. Trees and shrubs live by the God-given characteristics of nature based on what type tree or shrub they are. They all bloom and produce fruit in their season and their leaves turn whatever colors are designated for them to turn and drop when the time is right. Animals all live by instinct. When they are hungry, they hunt and eat, when they are tired, they rest, when their instinct tells them it is time to mate, they do– in whatever ritual God has ordained for them. Your Labrador retriever doesn't have a mental breakdown trying to figure out why he is a dog. He just lives out a dog life.

But man, only man has been given the power of reason and choice. Remember the tree of the knowledge of good and evil that scripture says was in the middle of the Garden of Eden was the center stage for the beginning of so much of the trouble that we experience still today in our lives–why was it there in the first place? If the fruit were so bad, why would it even be growing there? God planted it, why? The birds could nest in its branches they could even eat of the fruit. The fruit was never the issue. The tree was there because Adam and Eve had to have something to choose between. Their way or God's way. Love is not love unless it is chosen. There has to be something to choose between. Natural man, without the influence of God in his heart looks at something or someone and says, "Hmmm, that looks good, that would be enjoyable or profitable to have or experience," and he says, "I will have it," and then sets about to do so. In fact, so much so that James records in Chapter 1:14–15 how we are tempted when we see something that is so attractive and desirable that it "entices" us and actually draws us away ... ultimately to sin and death. These are the same thought processes and steps Adam and Eve took in the Garden of Eden plunging the whole world into darkness. You read it for yourself in Genesis Chapter 3. Eve is drawn to something that is desirable to her (and it wasn't just the fruit–it was the supposed promise that she would be "like God, knowing good and evil.") and she eats. Then Adam makes the same decision and he too is drawn away–from what? Drawn away from the right way, God's way, to some other path.

But man / woman with a new, a God-reborn heart, sees the same desirable thing and says, "Hmmm, that looks good, that would be enjoyable or profitable to have or experience," then because he has God's Holy Spirit dwelling in him/her another path of reason can set in. Now the power of choice can come into play. You and I can then realize, I cannot have that, in that way and walk in confidence before God. So we can make a choice and say, "I will not have it in that way and I will leave the fulfillment of satisfaction for that desire to God." It doesn't make the desire bad it just needs a right way to be satisfied.

Young children make decisions based solely on what they like and what makes them feel good. If you base your relational responses only on what you like and what will make you feel good, you are acting like and treating others like a child. And you thought having sex would be a sign that you were all grown up and mature. I Corinthians 13:11, "When I was a child, I talked like a child, I thought like a child, I acted like a child–when I became a man *(adult)* I put childish ways behind me." *(expanded text in parenthesis mine).* You become an adult when you act like one and make wise choices like one. Not when your driver's license says you've had enough birthdays.

It is said we can choose our actions, but we cannot choose the results. Often we make choices not recognizing the significance of our decision.

For example: Your buddy has a few beers and wants to show off his new wheels to his friends. He is more concerned with impressing the guys right now than with safe driving. He isn't paying attention and runs a stop sign. His car slams in to the side of another vehicle already in the intersection. The driver in the other car is killed. Now your buddy is facing manslaughter charges–when the action he chose was to just show off his stuff. The rest is results–often times out of our control.

Drugs, it's just a trial run, man. Alcohol/Cigarettes/Sex, all have an enticing appeal for what they bring to the table. "Give it a try, know for yourself what it is like and you can make wise choices."

Before we go too far, I want to give you a word picture that a friend by the name of Bob Stone has called the "Biological Hand Grenade Ladder." Here's the concept. We experience life at differing levels of emotional appetite and involvement.

We also have what can be called insatiable appetites, things and stuff that appeal to us, and no amount of having them quenches the desire to have them again and again. The problem or blessing, depending on how you look at it is that it requires an increasing level of that substance or experience to satisfy us. You give me one potato chip and I want more. In fact a whole advertising campaign was established on the concept, "Bet you can't eat one." It is because activities that stimulate our taste buds and especially our emotional taste buds become complacent with familiarity and demand more impulse for the same degree of enjoyment. Climb a small rock and you want to climb a bigger one. Jump a ditch and you want to try jumping a larger one to see if you can do it. Smoke a cigarette, drink a beer, have a joint, whatever—we crave more. The same is true with our sensual nerves and the way they are stimulated in our emotions. Think about the very first time you held hands with someone you enjoyed being with, and the first kiss. Depending on where you are right now in your degree of experience in this area, to think all you are going to ever do is hold hands doesn't exactly float your boat anymore. (If you are not there yet in your physical interaction experiences, don't worry, that time will come soon enough; just hear what is being explained and the full benefit of it will come in due time.) So each new level of expressing yourself in this way is like a higher rung on the ladder. Once you have experienced a particular rung for a while, the ones lower on the ladder are not such a big deal. They are merely a step toward the next rung.

Do you see why this can make dating someone who has been married before or who has lived with an opposite sex partner very volatile. They've been there, probably all the way up the ladder, and a peck on the cheek is just not the same buzz for them—even if it is still special for you. If you are not aware of this you can find yourself being encouraged to move more quickly up the ladder than you realize, or even skip some rungs and step up "to a new level of expression". When Mom and Dad are skeptical of you dating someone significantly older than you are, and want you to be very cautious, they do have a reason behind their madness. Is every person older than you out to take you down? No, but think beyond your present mentality here and realize some of the dynamics of which you may need to be aware.

Four

The Guys–Sons of Adam

I want to take a moment and pause the script and specifically acknowledge a group of friends that minister under an organization known as Ransomed Heart, based out of Colorado Springs, Colorado and headed up by John Eldredge. I have read most, if not all of John's books and listened countless times to tapes from one of their basic Boot Camp seminars as well as attended one in person. I call them friends, not because any of the guys on that team would recognize my name, but their hearts beat with my heart and I believe with the heart of the Father. They are already brothers, in Christ, only time and distance keep us from being true friends. There are a great number of thoughts that I have chewed on for so long that these guys address both in John's writings and in their seminar presentations and I can no longer separate where some thoughts came from, originally. That is not totally true. I am confident that John would acknowledge with myself, and the rest of his team, that all of truth originates in the heart of God and takes on its uniqueness as it is reflected by our individual stories and personalities. I say this so that as you read, if you are familiar with the ministry of Ransomed Heart, and you see something and think, "Man that sounds just like something

John Eldredge would say"–he may have, even though it is not shown in quotes in this material.

Back to the script ...

Who am I?

What gives me value?
What makes me feel important?

Why would anyone want me for a friend–
or want me to be their life's partner?

We all have questions we want and actually need answers for. Questions that we sometimes ask indirectly by our actions and our need for response. What are those questions that haunt us? Are our questions the same for guys and girls or are they different?

First of all, you need to know that God did not make generic human beings when He made you. He created you male or female and you are made in His image—uniquely masculine and uniquely feminine. In very different ways we each can reflect His nature. Man usually the more adventurous side–the warrior, the protector, with a wild and passionate heart. Ladies, you reflect more of the tenderness and merciful and compassionate side of His nature. Can a man be tender and a woman wild and passionate about life? Absolutely! However, the general nature of femininity is to nurture and be gentle, and the most often displayed characteristics of a man are his strength and boldness of spirit. And by strength, guys, I am not talking muscle here. I didn't understand this for a long time and since I never felt I was very strong (physically) as I was growing up I didn't often feel very powerful–not so.

Here it comes again.

> ## LIFE CONCEPT No. 1
>
> I LIVE MY LIFE BASED ON THE
> THINGS I BELIEVE TO BE TRUE.
>
> And I do that whether they are
> actually true or not!

So guess how I lived? Exactly, easily intimidated, seeking my "strength" and my identity from other peoples' responses and very seldom if ever choosing to be confrontational–even when needed. I would take a stand only when backed into a corner with no other choice.

Since I thought strength was associated with muscle power, I lived like I had no strength to offer, but I always wanted to. My dreams were of stepping up and being the hero. And all of my fantasies were "strong man" types where I hit the home run, or attacked the machine gun nest or ran the fastest race (like in the whole world ever). Many, many of you know exactly what I'm talking about. And, if you are honest with this you know I'm not just talking about little kid type dreams. Regardless of the number of your birthdays, you, like myself, still "dream" of being *The Man* or *The Lady* in many of life's situations. You will your whole life. It is a good thing!

But it does not have to only be a dream ...

THE GUYS

51

GUY'S BREAKOUT SESSION

*Ladies, your section follows right behind this one, but this next section is really intended to address the issues from a guy's perspective and I'm going to talk to them in "guy terms". It may or not make as much sense to you, but it is the way we think as guys and a lot of how we, as your male counterparts, approach our issues. You (ladies) can benefit by gaining some understanding of us if you choose to wade thru this portion with us–and you are welcome here. The choice is yours. Do pardon our "guy-ness".

Every man, no matter his age, has the same basic needs: To know that he is important, that he has value. That it matters that he lived. He wants to feel that his life has an impact that makes a difference. Think about almost any situation in life and you can see this played out at the deepest level of who we are and why we do what we do. Why does a guy feel good when he is the first one chosen for the make-up teams in his neighborhood or at school in PE, while the guy who is always the last one chosen feels embarrassed? Of course it is because of which guys are known to have the better skills for the particular game or activity. But it also says who is valued for his ability to help the team. One player is treated as more "important" and another feels he is very unimportant, and supposedly, has no value. What is the deep underlying emotion in road rage or many, many fight situations? At the heart of it is, "You can't treat me like that and get away with it–I am somebody too you know!" What is being said when one kid bullies another kid? Without a single word spoken the message is, "I'll prove to everybody that I have more value than you because I am powerful and can control you with my strength." What makes physical and sexual abuse in a family so devastating? The message is sent that in the place where you are known the best and should be loved the most, "you have no worth except as an object for my anger or my lust. You have no other importance here." We study, we pump iron, we strive to achieve something, so that someone will recognize our accomplishment and acknowledge that we have value.

John Eldridge in his book *Wild at Heart* says, "The deep question of a man's heart is, do I have what it takes?" That question comes in all forms and shapes, such as, "will I be able to stand when the battles, the struggles of life, come." Am I man enough, tough enough, brave enough, smart enough? But it is still the same basic question, "Do I have what it takes?" Do I have value here? Am I important as a person? These are not just one time questions, guys. You will be asking yourself these questions your entire life as situations arise and life comes at you new every minute of the day.

Relative to the relationships with our ladies our question can look like, "Will I have a beauty to win?" Will I have what it takes to fight for her, to protect her, to provide for her? Will there be a beauty that will even want *me* to be the one to rescue her, and will she feel secure in what I can offer her? Will she see me as having enough to be wanted by her? Will I be important to someone?

These questions are like mountains in the heart of a man, especially a young man. (But not necessarily limited to youthfulness.) They are huge!

For a while as we are growing up and maturing we will probably have other arenas than those filled with the ladies in which to attempt to find ourselves. Perhaps music or sports or art or outdoor activities or other adventures where we find a degree of success and decide we may just have what it takes after all. Those can be and should be not only fun, but good training grounds for later stages in life and preparation for the tougher battles that will come down the road. You have all heard or know from you own experience that there are many arenas where learning the disciplines of "hanging in there when the going gets tough" or "playing hurt" or "pushing through the tough part of a music recital or a project" are great lessons for life. Lessons that you can learn in debate squad or football or band that will have good applications all through life.

Eventually though, most of us, guys, will still turn to the ladies to check out how we measure up. I mean if she's a princess and she acts toward me as though I am the man, then I must be the prince, right? Great question!

But first who are these creatures we call the ladies, the daughters of Eve? And what relationship did God design for us together? She, woman, is the final activity of creation. She completes the design that God has for mankind to bear his image. Her tenderness and mercy, the essence of who she is in her femininity, all display a part of God's nature that a man generally does not demonstrate. She is the last of His creation, she is the final missing part—and when God is done with her, He decides even He needs a rest (Sorry ladies, only kidding). I mean she is really something!

What role does she play and what role do I play?

How strong is her allurement on us?

Think for a moment about the scene in the Garden of Eden as recorded in Genesis when Satan has come to Eve and she is tempted to question God's heart toward her and live in her own wisdom, and she eats of the forbidden fruit. We don't know how long it was. Scripture says in the first part of Genesis 3 "Adam was with her," seemingly right there beside her. Why he didn't do something when she was being tempted we don't know, but he did nothing! What we do know is that there was a period of time maybe no longer than "Here, try this," but there was at least a moment in time when Eve was fallen and Adam was not. Why did he eat? Why didn't he say, "No way, that goes against God's heart for us"? For sure, Adam was tempted to the desirability of the choice just as Eve was but there just may have been even more for him. John Eldredge recounts this story in his Wild At Heart seminars, and he suggests that Adam actually chose Eve over God.

"You've got to be kidding," you say. "Why would anyone do something that stupid?"

Oh really? So you have never placed a girl, or the response of one over God? Or a position on a sports team or the results of an art project or chair position in band as more important to you than God? I think John may be right. And guys, we have been looking up from our little boy worlds of soldier and football and computers ever since and seeing the daughters of Eve for the first time and saying within ourselves–Whoa!

First of all a man doesn't go to a woman to find the answer for his life, or his strength. He goes to her to *offer* his strength. You will never find the answer to your questions for who you are and do you have what it takes *from* Eve. She cannot give you your answer.

Femininity cannot bestow masculinity!

She is not the verdict on you! That truth alone could set some of you guys more free than you've ever imagined possible if you could realize, the response of a woman is not what makes you the man. I really like a statement that Dr. Laura Schlessinger uses on her talk show when she says to some guy who is trying to justify his less than admirable actions, "You were born a male, you have to make a choice to be a man." God made you with male gender. It is a choice to be what you were intended to be, a man!

Just as femininity cannot bestow masculinity, the response of society cannot bestow value, not at the deepest level of the heart. Oh we can make you feel special. We can even treat you like a king with our mock worship. You accomplish something of significance, especially something that is marketable as a talent or an item on the shelf, and as a society we will treat you like a god. We'll buy your tapes or your tennis shoes and we'll squeal and throw ourselves at your feet when you walk on stage or down the street. But in the deep recesses of your heart you will know that you cannot stop (whatever got you the popularity in the first place) or mess up. You have to keep on performing at least at the same level of perfection or we will drop you like a hot potato. We will replace you with the next "icon" wanna-be and we will forget you in a heartbeat!

Only the one who knows the true value of something can give value to that object. There is only one who knows your true value and how to bestow it on your heart. It is the one who created you. " … *I am fearfully and wonderfully made; your works are wonderful, I know that full well … your eyes saw my unformed body. All the days ordained for me were written in your book before one of them came to be*" (Psalms 139: 14, 16).

As a man's heart asks, do I have what it takes the biggest fear of a man's heart is ***failure.*** Not measuring up. Being exposed. Being found out as *not* having what it takes. Perhaps being laughed at. Falling short of what is expected of him. Having people we care deeply about be ashamed of us and embarrassed because of our unwillingness to pay the price, or our just not coming through in a given situation. Not being important. This very truth alone causes more of us than you could possibly imagine to hesitate when we should act. It causes us to shy away from situations where we might be exposed as failures. It causes us to not be willing to try at all. How many times have I said, "I'm not really thirsty right now" or "maybe later" when offered a drink or something to try that I really didn't want. I just didn't have the confidence to say, "No Thanks", and let the chips fall where they may. Why would I do that, why do you do that? We don't want to stand out, or appear weak or timid, or be "different". If we do we might not be as "welcome" as before and that might make me feel less valuable.

This fear of failure, or being found out can also cause us to react the opposite way from shy. It can prompt me to show off or act excessively tough, even against my own judgment or heart, to attempt to "prove" I have what it takes. It can make you willing to drive faster than you feel safe or even wise doing. You'll drink more than you could possibly want or treat someone in a way you would never treat them otherwise. More guys have probably climbed into bed or been "pushed" into the back seat of a car by their emotional need to prove they are not afraid of sex than ever wanted to be there. I did. The first time I went parking with a girl in the back seat of my buddy's car, I was not in love with her. Oh she was cute enough, but my pressure to make out was a pressure to "keep up", not seem weird, or heaven forbid, that anyone would think I didn't know how to kiss. It had nothing to do with romance at all. When I was in high school, I didn't date. Didn't really need to. (Didn't have the confidence to either.) I had a couple of buddies to run with that as I look back on it, they were my saviors in the way they included me in their lives and activities. They both had girl friends, most of the time, but they always made room for me. That allowed me to keep my "I Have Value" meter full enough through their incredible friendships that allowed me to not have to fake a lot of stuff to feel accepted (valued). Which was a good thing as I was very immature–or so it seems to me now.

When we are young we play army and cowboys and sports, or find any number of adventures to play the hero in. The wonderful thing in the world of fantasy and make believe is that we always *do have what it takes*. I've never lost a make believe battle (unless being captured or having to retreat for a while was the more courageous part). I never came in anywhere but first in the fantasy races I ran in or ball games I played in through make believe. I was the author of those scripts. I knew whom the bad guys were and where they were hiding or when the opposing team (which incidentally was never just an opposing team, they were really mean people that wanted to dominate the world if they won) was going to pull that trick play that I totally destroyed and scored the winning touchdown.

When we get a little older, hopefully our dreams involve more real things and real people. The most significant change for most of us as guys is when we begin to respond to the girls with something other than, "Yuck!" We not only begin to notice the girls but they, for most of us, become the next arena after our boyhood adventures to turn to for the answer to our "*do I have what it takes*" question. That is one reason girls are so "scary" to most of us at the early years of manhood. We think they hold the answer on us. It is like their response to us is the determining factor in our validation and defines our manliness. It doesn't, and they don't, but it can sure seem that way.

Because failing is one of our biggest fears as men, even as young men, guess what has become a readily available place to run to seeking a guaranteed "non failing" response from the girls? Good guess, if you guessed pornography. No wonder it has so many of us in bondage. First of all, pornography has absolutely nothing to do with true intimacy and romance. It is simply a manageable response arena, a place of adventure, where fantasy can guarantee the "success" of the viewer. It is a no risk arena, vulnerability wise. You cannot "fail"! That is why so many of us go there. But you need to know that the lie of this fantasy, especially as it plays out in your mind, is that the make believe story never has any *consequences* included in the script. Some hot sweet thing is going to say in the fantasy of your mind or over your phone or computer speakers the things you want to hear. She is going to say to you, "You are the man. You are important and so desirable and buff and you have what I want. And you can do just anything you want to do." Of course she is saying the same thing to 2 million other guys at the same time on their computer screen or from thousands of other magazine stands, but never mind that, you're special to her. Yeah right!

This fantasy road has an additional down side to it that I just want you be aware of. You never include in your fantasy the results of "being *her* man", and the impact that playing with her, even just in your mind has on your own heart, and your mind, and your future.

My future?

What's so bad about a little fantasy? It's just me and my little private world playing make-believe. Nobody gets hurt by that, right?

And you and I think we can absorb the pictures and the movies and the conversations and walk away with no scars–and we are wrong! To put it into scientific terms: Newton's Theory of Relativity says, "that for every action there is an equal and opposite reaction." That would translate directly into our conversation that for every action on our part there is a consequence, or equal and opposite reaction. That consequence is either good or bad depending on the action. There are not any neutral, no results, no consequent actions. When you play make-believe this way, and especially with sexual content, there are response patterns that you begin to establish in your mind, without even realizing you are doing so. Once set into the hard drive of your brain they are there for the rest of your life. Things that can show up much later in life when someone or some situation pushes the "recall button" for that stored material and the junk you put in—will be junk when it comes out. Period!

So what's the big deal? Why does our mind matter so much? "You could never imagine the myriad of thoughts that cross my radar screen on any given day," you say. Yes, I can. I don't have to know the specific details, but I've got a better picture than you might think. My radar screen bleeps too you know.

The big deal is because all of the actions you carry out now, or in the future, begin in your mind with a thought. Every great invention, every passionate act of love, every display of courage, every anything begins at some point, first, with a thought. Think about it (no pun intended). Our actions are actually a delayed announcement of what we have already been thinking. I know, I know, we all have blurted off at the mouth and said or done some spontaneous act that appeared, by any standard of wisdom, to have been done with no thought at all. That's not true. You may not have thought very long or well or smart, but you thought. The proof is because your mouth and your body would have done nothing without getting a signal from your brain to do it.

So what's my part as the guy, where do I have a place? You must first come to the realization that you are not what you do. You are who you are. What do I mean by that? As men, personality wise, we have a tendency, more than the ladies do, to gain our identity from our accomplishments. Meet a new group of guys at a party or most anywhere and we will introduce ourselves in some way by our positions in life or our accomplishments. This is especially true after we finish our formal education and begin working. While in school we say, or our friends will say things like, "Hi, I'm John." And our friends will add, or we'll find a "humble" way to share "He's the captain of our basketball team. Or he is first chair trumpet in the band or he dates that really cute girl in our math class." All of which in guy mentality are, accomplishments. When we graduate and begin work it sounds more like, "Hi, I'm John. I am with Knowles, Franks, and Johnson law firm" or, "Hi, I'm Sam. I am a computer design engineer with Gateway," etc. Again, that is what you do–it is not who you are.

Who you are is a young man *created in the very image of God* himself who … plays basketball, or trumpet, or dates the cutie in math class, or works as a lawyer or computer design engineer. Then, you break your leg and things go south in basketball or you get a new boss at work because someone younger than you got the promotion, or if that really cute girl in math class gets angry at you and bites your lower lip off so not only do you not date her anymore, you also can't play a note on your trumpet and you lose first chair position–you are still who you are. Your identity does not change just because your ability to perform does. (Get a handle on that truth early in life and you will never worry about a midlife crisis later. No extra charge!)

So why did God make us like we are? I mean why can't I enjoy playing house when I'm little and having tea parties like the girls do? Why is it so natural feeling and fun to tear things up and blow up stuff?

God created you to be dangerous!

He gave you a heart that is wild and courageous and adventurous.

Let me say that again. *God created you to be dangerous!* I know you have been told most of your life to be nice and straighten your room and watch your manners and be on time—and don't you dare get up from reading this book and run into the kitchen and say to your Mom, "This guy says I don't have to do those things anymore." You'll get us both killed!

What God wants you to know is that you were created for, and with, a purpose. To fulfill that purpose and be a success at this thing called life, as a man, will require a wild, and courageous, and passionate heart. Remember Life Concept No. 3?

LIFE CONCEPT No. 3

ALL OF THE CRUCIAL ISSUES OF LIFE
COME FROM THE HEART—
guard it above all else.

*Proverbs 4:23 says, "above all else
guard your heart for it is
the wellspring of life."*

Look all the way back in Genesis Chapter 1. God explained to Adam and Eve their purpose, and that was before they had disobeyed Him. He said in verse 28, " ... *be fruitful and increase in number; fill the earth and subdue it. Rule over the fish of the sea and the birds of the air, and over all the creatures that move along the ground.*"

Adam had, you have a mission, not a task—a mission. You and I have been given the privilege, the opportunity, the responsibility as men of impacting the world we live in, for good! It is why you have been given the strength you have. Not so you can thump your younger siblings or some guy in school who is physically smaller than you are, but so you can use it for good and bring your power to bear where it will be needed and helpful. This mission, this calling of your heart in many, many ways is going to take on all the aspects of a battle. In fact you are already in a battle right now whether you realize it or not. This book, this information that you are either embracing or frowning at in disbelief is a part of a battle–a battle for your own heart. And in this battle you have an enemy. One who is playing for keeps, and he has one simple itty bitty agenda. That is to destroy your confidence before God, and in God so you will doubt God's heart toward you. If he (Satan) can get you to doubt that God's heart toward you is good and can be trusted no matter what things appear, you will wonder if He (God) is not holding out on you and making you miss some of the really fun stuff. Can you imagine how that might play out in the context of sexual purity and abstinence?

Do you have what it takes for life, for this battle? God wants you to know that…

He has given you what it takes!

"And God is able to make all grace abound to you, so that in all things, at all times, having all that you need, you will abound in every good work" (2 Corinthians 9:8).

You do have what it takes because He gave it to you, and continues to give you what you need for every situation (including guarding your heart in this area of romance and response!) Again, notice that I did not say it requires you to be strong or have great physical strength. Don't think for one instant that if you are not physically muscular or tall or buff that you don't have a place in God's larger story.

God looks at the heart, He has all the physical power He needs, and will give you what you need, but you have to bring your heart along yourself. He will leave that decision to us. Remember, you and I live by choice.

And if you *are* physically strong, I mean you can press huge pounds or run with the wind or leap tall buildings, by the world's standards, you will be called on for no more, and no less a part in this adventure. Those who will succeed in this conflict will be strong in their trust of God's heart and they will walk in the power of His (God's) might. We are all called out to be good stewards of our physical temples (our bodies). Physical strength and exercise are not bad, don't be silly, just don't put your trust there to get you through.

But what about this wild and dangerous heart thing? Most guys have stories to tell of when they have been dangerous, wild, off the charts. Maybe in drama or athletics or some other arena, or maybe just what you are willing to try, or take a dare to do. Those are adventures for sure but they are what would fall into a category referred to as *casual* adventures. They have a place, and often times they are fun and as we mentioned earlier they have a good purpose. We can even learn from them.

They are not the issues of life!

Guys, most of the time we are dangerous for nothing. We do stuff that is dangerous, but it has no significant value other than just to do it. To prove to yourself or to someone else that you can, or will, do whatever.

God's creation of your wildness of heart was so that you could be:

Dangerous for Good!

God wants to call you out, and up. Into something that is bigger than you are, bigger than you have imagined–His larger story! It is a story that is bigger than life. It will outlast your physical life and at times require more than you have to give, unless you allow Him to empower you to live it. And a part of that story *will involve* the way you interact and treat the ladies, but it is so much more.

Remember my saying earlier that growing up I never felt that I was physically strong, so I would often not feel confident competing with the other guys in attempting to do some sports activity or daring act. While I loved sports, I played in the band in high school. I liked music, and still do, but most of my choices were made the way they were because I didn't think I could successfully compete. But guess where I could compete? That's right, I could be very successful competing for the response of the ladies. And so I learned how to "listen" and be the nice guy. I learned what it meant to be "sensitive and caring". It wasn't too tough to be successfully strong, masculine wise, when compared to the girls. (Well, most of them, my girl friend in the 5th grade could whip every guy in my grammar school, which came in handy at the time.)

I mentioned earlier that a guy doesn't go to a girl to find his strength but to offer it to her. So what would be an example of what it would look like for a guy to "offer" his strength to the girl rather than asking her to validate him somehow? Let me attempt to show you from a dad with two beautiful daughters' perspective:

You know what I expect from a guy who dates my daughters? First of all I expect him to come to me and find out what

I expect. I want to know that he knows that when he walks out of the door of my house with her, he is assuming my roll–at least for the short period of their time together.

What is my roll as her Dad, the man in her life (at least while she is living at home)?

Protector and Provider.

So what should he do? The guy.

He is to protect her, at all costs. That would mean he is not to subject her to unnecessary danger by where he takes her or how he acts with her or toward her. He is not to put her at risk by how he conducts himself or put himself in such a condition where he cannot carry out his protective responsibilities toward her. He is to provide the leadership and direction for the evening. He doesn't have to dictate all the choices, but be responsible for seeing that the necessary choices are made. [Like places where her father would and would not take her himself. (Would her dad have brought her to this movie or this party?) He must be willing to decide what they will and will not do and whether or not those choices honor her–which ultimately also honor her father. Would her dad let her drink, smoke, try this–whatever *this* is? And what time is her expected return and then be responsible for making it happen.] That is one perspective of a man *offering* his strength on behalf of the lady.

Let me throw out another perspective to think tank on:

Gang Rape: Don't raise your hands on this one but has anybody here ever participated in a gang rape? No, I mean it–really!

I have, and I'm not bragging. Oh not like you think of at first maybe. But watch.

You take out this neat, cute young lady and you have a great time. I mean she's a cutie, and fun to be with and everything. And, at some point in the evening you decide to test the waters to see how far you can get (I'm sorry, to see if she likes you). You don't push your luck and all you do is hold hands and you try and get a goodnight peck on the cheek. Fair enough.

Next guy up. Remember the biological hand grenade ladder; our level of desire doesn't get the same buzz out of lower rungs of familiar stuff. After a date or two she is getting more comfortable with holding hands and pecks on the cheek thanks to the "handsome" first guy in the "gang" so Guy No. 2 may get a better good night kiss. She wants intimacy too you know, it's written on her heart just like it is on yours. She wants to know if she is delightful and you send the message that oh yeah, "you are delightful—and here is how you can tell, pucker up baby!" Nice move slobber lips!

Gang member No. 3 shows up on the scene. And maybe all this progression takes place over several months or even several years or maybe in one week, but her comfort level is being expanded and she begins to understand that her "desirability" response is conditioned by her stepping up on the next rung of the ladder.

This next Guy is a real needy guy and he doesn't care who pulls his trigger or who gets burned in the process, he has a need to prove himself and a reputation to keep—and she is going down. (Remember, he is desperately trying to answer his own question, in the wrong places.) Maybe it isn't Guy No. 3. Maybe it takes No. 4 or 5 or 6 to progress her along the rungs of the ladder, but the end result is she gets raped. By the time No. 6 slides in beside her, she may even be agreeable to sharing this place on the ladder with him and you would say, "She didn't have to go all the way." Chances are you're right, she made choices along the way just like the guys did—but in fact she didn't go all the way with *him*. Each guy undressed her defenses one step at a time through her need for being noticed and her God-given design for intimacy. And believe me, she had no intention of going there when she was asked by Guy No. 1 to hold hands.

Is it any less rape than if all the guys came together at the same time and forced themselves on her? Then at least she would have fought—now she embraces. Is this analogy extreme? You decide, but before you blow it off and go looking for your next rung on the ladder, read:

Matthew 18:6

"But If anyone causes one of these little ones who believe in me to sin, it would be better for him to have a large millstone hung around his neck and to be drowned in the depths of the sea."

And then

In Matt 25:40, "The King will answer and say to them, "Truly I say to you, to the extent that you did it to one of these brothers (sisters) of Mine, even the least of them, you did it to Me." NAS (parenthesis expansion mine).

Be very careful here guys. Are you really prepared to give God an answer for why you treated his daughters like expendable toys, something to play with—just to attempt to satisfy your own ego and impulses?

In Mark 10:19 God says we are not to (now here's a word you don't hear very often) *defraud* each other. That simply means we are not to be deceptive or deceitful. In this context it means that we are not to do things or treat someone in such a way so as to create a desire for passion in the other person that we cannot satisfy in a God honoring way. That is not talking about our "lust" for them or their response to us. It is referring to turning them on so that they want us–big time. Then we cannot satisfy their want in a way that honors God, and ultimately them, or you.

You want a classy lady, one who is deeply beautiful and stands strong in life? One who will honor you as a man? Who wants to understand you for who you are as a man and wants you to be all God wants for you? Then step up and *be* the man, not the stud, the man. This kind of lady is not going to be interested in less. She can tell when you are coming to her hoping to prove your strength, or whether you are coming to her to offer the strength of who you are. Offer your strength to her in ways that will point her to God and let Him give her to whomever is best for both of you.

Ask yourself this question, "What is your heart toward her, what do you really want *for her*–not *from* her—*for her*?" Go to her with that.

Every guy wants his life to be an adventure worth living out. With dreams and goals and anticipation of what is yet to come. A life that makes a difference that he was born and impacts the world he lives in. A girl wants to be invited to join you in *your* adventure, the one God is taking you on. She doesn't want to *be* the adventure or be treated like one. It sounds fun to be someone's every thought, but the fun gets old and boring quick–even for the girl.

Guys, what if God should move our hearts to do something very different here? What if we dare to offer our strength to the girls you interact with? What if we make a commitment to give our strength to them to help them realize God's best for their lives? Then instead of being a part of the problem, we become big brothers in Christ? Now don't just say, "uh-huh" and be casual with this. Know that it is God's heart toward his daughters that they be all He created them to be, but be careful that this is your heart as well. This may be the toughest thing you have ever done. This might mean you have to find yourself, figure out who you are, some other way than by the responses of the ladies. For some of you–no big deal–you've got your other personal "loves" where you get your strokes. Maybe it's your grades or sports or how well you play a musical instrument or sing (anyway, that's a whole another subject). But for most of us, it will be like learning to breathe a new way. It might mean we have to look again at the reasons why we strut our stuff and flex our manliness in the ways we usually try to.

> *Guys: Turn to the girl sitting next to you, if there might be one right now and say, "I can't let you read this next part. It is way too personal to me as a guy, and I want to process it alone."*

Now that she is not looking…

There are a couple of things that God has shown me that have helped make a major difference in my understanding of the allurement that the ladies have on us as guys.

Get this one truth and the time it took to read this whole book will not have been a waste of your time even if you get nothing else.

Beauty, the very essence of it is designed into your manness to capture you, to awe you and draw you to it, and to hold you. It is a part of what pulls your heart toward God. If a man is an adventurer only, by that I mean he has got to have the next big thrill or experience, he must keep the adrenaline level peaked out. Or if he is always looking for a battle to fight just for the sake of being in a battle–he is a needy, shallow man. Sure we crave the rush of adventure and there is nothing as exhilarating as having something worth fighting for–that is what beauty does–it gives purpose to the battles and adventures. Beauty is most often something outside of you. A man is not generally thought of in terms of "beauty" or being beautiful. A sunset is, or a majestic landscape is, music perhaps, a wild animal, a nice car, or any number of things depending on how your heart is wired to see beauty. But every man at even very young ages recognizes, on sight, beauty in a woman without any instructions or tutoring or anything, except there she is! Sit at a distance and watch a group of guys, almost any age group of guys, just guys. They will be slamming on each other and telling stories of exaggerated accomplishments, and then let an attractive lady walk past, and just watch. Generally for a moment the entire conversation or activity of the group will stop, and to the man we will sort of "catch our breath" and look, until we realize everyone else in the group is gawking too and we get embarrassed. Then we start giggling and punching on each other for getting so easily caught up.

Why? How do they do that to us? Well first of all God designed *you* that way, *she* is not. The ladies in your world do see and recognize beauty, but not in the same way you do as a man.

Hint No. 1: There are very few things in your whole life that you will see and process the same way that the girls in your life will see and process things. She is a compliment to us, not a clone.

Back to the beauty thing. By her very God-given design she, the daughter of Eve, is beautiful to us, in ways a landscape or music sonata can never display. It is good. She is an image of beauty itself.

She is not *the* beauty! She is a reflection of *the beauty*.

That is not a slam on her, she is incredible–she is not the whole story. You treat her in your mind and in your heart as the whole story and it will eat your lunch. God is the whole story. His beauty and majesty and power are awesome, and are enough to capture and hold your heart in worship forever.

Look at this:

For since the creation of the world God's invisible qualities—His eternal power and divine nature—have been clearly seen, being understood from what has been made, so that men are without excuse. For although they knew God, they neither glorified Him as God nor gave thanks to Him, but their thinking became futile and their foolish hearts darkened. Although they claimed to be wise, they became fools and exchanged the glory of the immortal God for images made to look like mortal man and birds and animals and reptiles. Therefore God gave them over in the sinful desires of their hearts to sexual impurity for the degrading of their bodies with one another. They exchanged the truth of God for a lie, and worshipped and served created things rather than the Creator—who is forever praised. Amen!

Romans 1:20–25 NIV

The ladies in your world are image bearers of His beauty—enjoy her, eventually love her—don't worship her.

Man Secret: In the movie "Finding Forrester", Jamal Wallace, a young gifted kid growing up in the Bronx is befriended by, and he becomes a friend to an older man, a reclusive author who wrote one book, a Pulitzer prize winning novel, and then hid himself away in an apartment as a result of some very painful losses in his life (the loss of a brother that was killed in a car accident even after surviving the dangers of World War II). As their friendship grows, William Forrester shares this insight about women with Jamal—and it is priceless!

It is this, *"An unexpected gift at an unexpected time."*

Birthdays, anniversaries (for every imaginable event there is), Christmas, whatever. Those are fun occasions (that every girl remembers, and most guys forget). Gifts or flowers or candy or a special activity are good ideas. But, if you want to make some major mileage with a lady, "*an unexpected gift at an unexpected time.*" Bank on it!

I want you to take some time. Some real time. Put this material down and enter into a covenant of silence with those around you or the activities you are raring to get to. For the next 15 minutes, or longer if God leaves you there, take some solitude time and get alone with God and ask Him, for yourself, what His take on this is. Ask him what He had in mind when he made you and where He wants you to step up into the larger story–and while you've got Him on the line ask Him what He wants you to offer to the ladies in your world. You might even thank Him for the beauty they bear image of–that is true worship!

Now go ...

Five

The Ladies–Daughters of Eve

*This section for the girls only

However, *gentlemen*, just like with the girls relative to your chapter, it could be very wise for you male gender types to look into the heart of the most mysterious creature God ever created, if you dare! No man–no man–No Man, understands them fully; and that would include the one writing this chapter. But I do believe I have been blessed to live with and around some classy women in my life, and they have taught me long and hard.

Now ladies,

Thank you for being patient and allowing us guys to process some information ahead of you in our previous section. The more courteous protocol would be for the ladies to be allowed to go first. I won't speak for all of the guys reading this, but most of us as men need to be put in a slower group when it comes to "getting it" relative to this relationship thing, and I thought it wise to give us as much head start as possible.

So if guys and girls are different, and we are, then what would be *the* question of a girl's heart? Does she have a feminine version of the guys "Do I have what it takes?"

The question of the feminine heart is:

> Am I lovely?
>
> Do you notice me?
>
> Am I captivating to you?

These questions strike at the need we all have to feel important, valued, and loved. They are the feminine version of the same universal questions that we all want an answer for.

Ladies, you ask those questions in as many ways as there are individuals out there, but it is the thread that runs through a very lot of what you do and how you go about it—especially relative to us guys.

And yes, I do realize that there are many, many arenas where you can attempt to find yourself. Activities and ways to prove to yourself and to others that you do have value and importance, that you are lovely. As you strive and excel in music or sports or art or business we will idolize you. You can even excel at nothing except in being willing to show off the God-given figure you have been blessed with and we will swoon at your feet. But in your heart of hearts you will not feel secure because of these accomplishments. You know as well as I do that if you find your value in your performance, or in your looks, you have to keep getting better at performing and physically looking good (heaven forbid if you put on a few pounds, or get a zit). You stump your toe on this, or get caught in the rain so you don't have perfect hair or, God forbid, let your tan fade, or simply get older; and as a society we will leave you in the dust running after the next hot "body" and pretty face. It is a sad commentary on how fickle we can be as a society, but you know it is true. You see it every day.

The sports, the music, art, crafts, beauty pageants, there is nothing inherently wrong in pursuing and really pouring yourself into them. All of these arenas and many more like them are great avenues for developing skills and confidence and identifying things that are a natural "fit" for you. Some of you may well find your life's calling in these early adventures–the very things you were made for. But they are not you! They are what you do. Who you are is an image bearer of the Most High God. It is He who made you with all of your glory and worth.

You may find that you are really good in softball, or tennis, or golf, or with a musical instrument or whatever, and you really enjoy playing. You may even be good enough that you could pay your way through college with scholarships and possibly even turn pro. By the very way we as a society will respond to you; you will gain a certain level of identity (value). But if you blow out your knee and your sports days are over, or if your hearing fades as a result of an inner ear infection and any hope of a musical career fades with it, you have not *devalued* all of a sudden. I know, the rest of us will soon forget you (at least in the way we elevated you before) but you have lost none of your true worth. Yes, you may find yourself going in another direction than you thought originally and perhaps even struggle for a while in finding a new path for your life, but you are still **you**–and that **you** is good!

Hear me on this one. You are, whether you can see it or not, the very image of beauty. Yes you! I don't care if anyone points it out or not, or even if anyone else notices. In your very design by God himself you are a reflection of beauty. *The true beauty*. His beauty. You are not *the beauty*, not yet anyway, but a reflection of the true beauty that will not fade with age or become so familiar as to no longer be noticed.

Just a note to you personally from the heart of this guy:

> You capture the heart of a man with the essence of who you are. God designed you that way, and He designed us guys to notice. You don't even have to put on a show to make us look. Think for a moment and remember there have been times and cultures where the girls and women covered up a lot more than you do today. Some even covered their heads and they didn't have highlighting and hair straighteners or eight "gazillion" options of makeup and eyeliners. There was a time they didn't even have mirrors (that may have been a blessing, I don't know). Hint: Ladies, the show you do put on is actually more to compete with the other girls for which ones we will look at, not whether or not we will look. Trust me—we will look!

Go with me for a moment to somewhere near the beginning as it is described in scripture in the book of Genesis and recap together the progression of creation. Watch how it becomes more and more refined and rises to its conclusion. First there is darkness and all is void and without form, then God separates the light from the darkness, then the waters part and form the sky and then the land. Next comes the plants and animals, everything that lives upon the face of the earth. Then He (God) creates man, one who is made in the very image of the Creator. One who is given the authority and responsibility of subduing the earth and ruling over it. Wow, what a creature! Then there seems to be a pause in His work as He reflects upon all that He has made—to which everything He has said, "It is good."

Then comes the first "Not good."

In Genesis 2:18 God says that it is "not good for the man to be alone", that the man needs a helpmate (and all the ladies said, "Amen"). A helpmate who by her very design can help complete the image of the Creator as it is born out in mankind. And God takes a rib from Adam's side and creates Eve. And *she, **you**,* are like the crowning glory of Creation. She bears the image of God in ways Adam most likely cannot.

Most of you know the next part of the story recorded in Genesis Chapter 3. Eve is tempted and ultimately begins to doubt the heart of God toward her. She believes *the lie,* and she takes the fruit they have been commanded not to eat and tastes it. She then turns to Adam and offers the fruit to him, and he makes his own choice and tastes it as well. Something very unwanted happens. Remember how we can choose our actions but we cannot always choose the results or consequences? Scripture says they actually died (at the level of the heart) as a result of the choice they made. Now the roles we were created to play aren't so clear anymore. Reflect for a moment longer on the scene in the Garden of Eden there was a moment in time when Eve had fallen, and Adam had not. How long, we don't know. Scripture seems clear that Adam was right there with Eve when she ate, so maybe it was no longer than, "here try this." But there was at least some amount of time when Adam could still have made a different choice than Eve made. Why did Adam eat the fruit? He didn't have to. He knew what God had warned would happen if they did eat it. John Eldredge in his Wild at Heart Boot Camp sessions suggests that Adam actually chose Eve over God.

"You have got to be kidding," you say. "Why would any-one do something that stupid?" Oh really? So you have never even for a moment entertained the thought of how wonderful it might be to be so beautiful and enticing that a guy would choose you over everything else–even God? And certainly you have never placed a guy, or the response of one as the highest priority in your life? And assuredly not a position on a sports team or debate squad or chair position in band–God, and only God, as our first priority, right? Whatever!

And ladies, let me be vulnerable again, we guys have been *wowed* by you ever since God introduced you to us in the garden. There are times when we still choose you over God. That's not always your fault, but you play a very important role based on your response and what you offer to us to try–just like in the garden a long, long time ago. So don't put your righteous hat on too quickly. You are not without participation here. Eve ate first.

Because of how God made you and because of the way we, guys, look at you, you have incredible influence. Make your influence on us for good. Be very careful how you treat God's sons. Don't treat us as response meters to check out how you're doing. As guys we are visual in our appetites. Be sensitive to that when you select your outfits. Sure, you show it off, and we'll look. And you will give account to your Heavenly Father for your assistance in helping cause us to stumble in our hearts.

Matthew 18:6, " But If anyone causes one of these little ones who believe in me to sin, it would be better for him (her) to have a large millstone hung around his (her) neck and to be drowned in the depths of the sea." (Parenthesis expansions mine)

When I see a girl all decked out from head to toe, I can guess 90% of the time from all the way across the parking lot what she dressed for today. If she is "style", I mean every piece and accessory fine tuned to the nth degree, I know she is dressed to compete with the girls she is meeting somewhere or that she thinks she might run into. She does not want to come up lacking. But if she has on her "camo", her hunting clothes, with as much skin showing as she dare risk and still get out of the house, or as tight as she can fit into and still breath, I know she is looking for the response of the guys. And this is pretty consistent whether she is thirteen or thirty and beyond.

Please don't misunderstand what I am saying with this: we love it when a lady is dolled up and looks like a million bucks. Every guy loves it when you are looking fine! To me though, the real test of attractiveness is after about three days of no makeup or hair driers on a backpacking or mission trip, living out of a tent. If she is confident then, in simply who she is, without all the "helpful" paraphernalia–my, my, my! That, ladies, is cute! Or dress her to the limit and *then* let her get caught in the rain because of a flat tire. God definitely knew what he was doing when He created you.

Ladies, it is a wise maiden who learns that there is a difference, and knows how to tell the difference, when a guy is coming to you *with* his question to attempt to validate his strength (value), or when he is coming to you to *offer* who he is with his strength. Be careful in this, it is a pretty heady thing to be the focus of some guy's attention, for a short while. But you will bore with this quicker than you think. And maybe you could even be the one a guy comes to *for* validation. "Do I have what it takes," he asks with his actions and gestures and desires for response. These are questions that only God can answer for him, so you had better be up to the task of being God if you are going to attempt to fill God's shoes.

You were never intended to be able to give a guy the answer to his heart question. Let God grow them up to be the men you dream about and can follow and serve alongside. You become the godly Lady that this man among men is going to notice for your character and wisdom. He won't miss your beauty, it just will not be all that he sees.

Great you say, just what I have always wanted the boys to think of when they see me in the hall at school. "There goes real godliness and wisdom, wow!" Yeah right! Let me clue you in on something else then, it would nauseate most of you to know what we do think of when we look at you. Just leave some room for the possibility that we think very differently than you may perceive we do.

Everything, I mean everything, is something to play with in the mind of 99% of the young men you know. You think commitment and relationship. We think conquer and enjoy. You think soul mate. We think adventure. You think romance and intimacy. We don't think. Depending on the age of the people you fit in with right now it might help you to know that as guys we go through stages of maturing that are quite different than you do as ladies. There is a phase in a guy's mind and heart somewhere in the middle teen and early twenties that we are more like cowboys and adventurers than we are husbands and dads. It's not bad, that's where we learn a lot about who we are as guys. Somewhere along our path of development near the end of the cowboy stage we tend more toward the warrior and lover stage of our life. This is a good progression of maturing as you will want us to be willing to step up to both if we should have a relationship at some point.

However, if a man acts and wants to treat you like a lover, when in reality he is still living only in the adventure stage of his life—you have a great picture of today's sex mentality.

Ladies, forgive my bluntness, but often times to us, the guys, "romance" at this adventure stage in our lives, is just one more fun ride. And whether you want to accept it or not, that is the real motive in some of our actions, however "nice" we wrap them. You can be, and for some of us are, nothing more than an adventure. How many of you ladies really and truly want to be thought of and treated like a disposable toy? Nothing more than a thing to be played with and tossed aside for the next guy to play with?

None! Not really.

I'm not trying to be insensitive here, nor am I trying to paint some ugly picture of men. We too are image bearers. God saw all that He had made and said it was good. But we are wired different than you are. Can we, as men, be sensitive and caring and make lasting commitments and be worth keeping yourself for?

Absolutely!

Just keep in mind that in the world we are brought up in, you are way ahead of most guy thought processes when it comes to commitment, especially in relationships. We guys mature slower in this area, sometimes into our late twenties or even early thirties before we know who we are enough to be able to give ourselves away to you. To allow you to be the receiver of our love and strength rather than trying to help us *prove* we have love and strength. Without meaning to be crass, it is the difference in our being a lover or a consumer. (I know, that is not a very pretty picture.)

Do I mean you can't find a guy less than thirty years old that is worth having? You know better. I said go in with your eyes wide open on the time frames when most of us can really begin to give ourselves away to you and not just take from you. Ask Jean, my wife, what are some of the ways you will be affected by being in a relationship with a guy who doesn't know who he is yet? "What a chore," she would tell you. She put up with a lot before I began to really understand who I am and where my true value and identity come from enough to see and love who she really is, and who she is not. She is not the answer on my life. She doesn't want to be. In fact she still puts up with a lot, because I'm still a work in process—I'm not Christ-like yet. But you already knew that, right?

Remember the question of the feminine heart? "Am I lovely?" "Do you notice me?" "Am I captivating to you?" This question lends itself to create the biggest fear in a woman's heart?

The fear of abandonment.

If I cannot "hold" you with who I am and how I respond to you, you might leave. And it will prove I must not be lovely enough or maybe I'm not captivating at all. There is no other logical reason why some women tolerate and accept the things they do from guys except they are afraid he'll leave and they won't have anyone. Some of you know personally what I'm talking about, or you know someone who it just makes no sense why they keep taking the treatment they get from some guy. Now you know. She is attempting to answer her heart's question from the wrong sources. Just like we guys do. Just like you do if you don't understand the need behind the questions.

Do you notice me? Am I desirable? Am I worth fighting for? Do you find me captivating enough not to leave me for someone or something else? Abandonment slams on all of those questions. Some of you think you can give a guy all he asks for and you won't get left. Wrong! You cannot give a man what he needs. What he needs is to validate his masculinity, and **you** can't do that for him. God guaranteed it.

Ladies—Princesses—Daughters of Eve, we do not have the answer for your life questions any more than you have ours. God alone has your answer. Ask Him who you are and what He had in mind when He formed you. It just might blow you away to find out you have been thinking way too small of yourself.

So how are you going to act toward us guy image bearers? What do you do if you can't live with us and you don't want to live without us? Be all *you* can be in Christ. Focus your heart to grow in Christ and become the woman that a godly man is going to take notice of. Your Abba Father and his Abba Father wants to give you both good gifts, the guys are being encouraged to become the men of God that your Abba Father can entrust with you. You become the godly gift He will want to present to them. Remember, there is a larger story going on here than just you and "Mr. Right" (whomever he might be).

Question:
What if, just what if, you choose to give up your hot seat of being pursued and posing for our attention and become the biggest cheerleaders we could ever hope to have to become the warriors for good that God created us to be? That instead of being a part of the problem you become our Sis' in Christ?

Now don't just say uh-huh and be casual with this. Know that it is God's heart toward his son's that they be all He created them to be, but be careful that this is your heart as well. This may be the toughest thing you have ever done. This might mean you have to find yourself, figure out who you are, get your security some other way than by the responses of the boys. For some of you that will be no big deal. You've got your other personal "security blankets" where you get your strokes (and that's an entire subject of its own). For others it may well be like learning to breathe a new way, just like it was for the guys. It might mean you have to look again at the reasons why you strut your stuff and show a little skin in the ways you usually do.

Let me offer my own opinion on what has been the most drastic change in our society in my lifetime. Ladies, I confess, we guys have always been opportunists, always looking for a pretty face and a fun time. We have always been the consumers and we would willingly consume anyone we could that would make us feel "manly" or whatever. Fortunately, most of you ladies presented quite a formidable obstacle by being quite hard to consume. Distant, court me, pursue me, earn my attention and affection kind of obstacles. But somewhere along the way, in the last number of years, the girls entered the hunt. And we guys just kept on consuming, only now with no roadblocks to slow us down. In fact if we don't pursue fast enough, we get caught from behind by some chic out looking for her own good time. Maybe trying to answer her own questions for validation with any "boy toy" she can capture. I'm not saying it's all your fault that our society is promiscuous, we guys have never been anything but a part of the problem. I'm just saying that you opened the flood gates that we as "make my day" opportunistic, egocentric, males have let you join us in the chase—to both our ruin.

In some ways we need you to wait in the tower for us to come rescue you from the terrible dragon. There are knights in your world who are willing to storm the castle, to risk their lives for you, fair maiden, but not for long if they find out the princess has gone out drumming up her own dragons.

Re-read Matthew 18:6, *"But If anyone causes one of these little ones who believe in me to sin, it would be better for him to have a large millstone hung around his neck and to be drowned in the depths of the sea."*

Stop reading for just a moment to clear the area around you. The immediate area of any guys.

If you happen to be reading this in a small group setting, or if your boyfriend is sitting on the couch beside you, tell him or the guys in the group to go get a life, these next few statements are for you alone.

Now,

Let's step off the treadmill for a moment and let me share something with you as ladies that can make a very large difference in how you respond to the men in your world.

When God created us as men, He made us in very particular (your take on that might be, weird) ways. You already know we are "unusual" at times and that we are wired and process information differently than you do. All that left brain-right brain, logical vs. relational thing. And for all of its potential for frustration to you, our differences are good. You don't have to take my word for it. God made us male and female, and upon observation of the finished products said, "It is good!" Anyway, one of the primary ways we are different from you is in our aggressiveness and strength and warrior mentality. That is also part of what makes us attractive to you. Every woman longs for a valiant prince who will come for her and fight for her and protect her and ultimately provide for her. No girl dreams of a prince that is afraid of his horse and runs at the first sign of danger. Or one who will not fight for her because he is afraid he might get hurt. Admittedly there needs to be more to the picture than killing the bad guys and riding off into the sunset together. If that is all there is to the story there are major puzzle pieces missing, such as his ability to love you and cherish you and enjoy you. Many of you come into a relationship with a guy looking for these things, the valiant prince characteristics. The desire for those characteristics is wired into you from birth. That is good!

The problem comes when you believe we are **The Protector** and **The Provider** and **The Lover** that can satisfy your desires and give you that lasting sense of security. We are not. I sometimes wish we were. I know at times in my life I have tried to fake it and act like I was the one, because it can get some incredible response if you ladies buy into it. But hear it again. We, the men, are a *reflection* of The Strength, The Provider, The Lover–we are not the source.

God alone is! Always has been! Always will be!

Can we offer our strength to you–absolutely, and we should. Can we give our very physical life to protect you–no doubt (at least you shouldn't have reason to doubt that we would). Are we to be a source of providing for you, and love and acceptance and joy for you, and with you? Now we are getting there! We are and should be a channel of those very things that can come to you from The Source. No more, and no less. We can never make you totally secure or loved or satisfied. And you cannot for us either. Thank goodness!

Enjoy us, love us, be the woman that causes the man in us to want to be The Man. Don't elevate us to little god status.

Take some time to get alone with God and seek His heart on this matter of how you should treat the guys that come into your world. What should you take from them and what should you offer? But the toughest question you will ask, whether you have the nerve to admit it or not is, "God, what is your heart toward me, can I trust you with this matter of relationships and sending someone my way or do I have to go get him?" Take some real alone time and let your Heavenly Father show you His heart, and then yours, and decide with Him where to go from here.

Begin with the End in Mind

Only as we really begin to understand and remember that there was a story going on before we were born, and that there will be a story continuing after we are gone, and that it was God's plan from the beginning that you and I be invited to join in that story, will we be able to keep this whole relational thing in context. I still have to constantly remind myself when I am struggling, that this thing, this issue, this moment (whatever it is), as huge as it may seem, is still only a piece of the story–just a part that must somehow fit into the whole.

There is a saying that applies very well here and actually is good wisdom in many areas of life:

> "Begin With The End In Mind."
>
> If you want to be successful at most anything–we are wise to begin with the desired end result in mind.

You want to become a great violinist or concert pianist, practice and approach every part of it with the end in mind.

Ever thought about winning a state championship in sports: football, basketball, soccer, you name it—then train, practice, play with the desired end result in mind.

What do you want out of this relationship thing? The best approach would be to begin now with the end in mind. What do you want *for* the girl or guy you find yourself attracted to, begin now with the end in mind. What do you want the message of your life to be when it is said and done, begin with the end in mind.

What do you mean, "begin with the end in mind?" Okay, let's say six months, or six years from now, you actually get the guy or the gal you set your heart on. And you look back and can say, "Wow, I had to be a slut to do it, but I got him!" Or, "Boy, she was sure a good catch no matter what I had to compromise to get her." That is such a wonderful foundation for a great long lasting relationship, huh? How long will you be willing to continue to compromise, or be the slut to attempt to keep him or her? If you want to be able to feel secure in the heart of the one God has given you and trust yourself to him or her with the real person of who you are—begin with the end in mind.

Now I know, and you know, we can take in all of this information and any number of facts about the nature of guys or girls and what part our parents play in our lives and what we should and should not do, and even why we should or should not do it. But reading about and discussing this entire concept of living from our hearts will have been pretty much a waste of our time unless we all recognize our total inability to live this out in our own strength. You can't–I can't! We won't even want to! The pull is too strong and the fruit looks soooooo good.

So if attempting to "sample" all the options that appear available is not a wise plan, how do I go about determining who is The Guy or The Girl and what part do I play other than sit at home and wait for prince charming to call? What if I am someone's Prince Charming, how do I figure out whom I am supposed to call?

I like what Joshua Harris said in his book, *Boy Meets Girl*, "God knows all things. He knows whom we'll marry before we meet him or her. But that doesn't mean our task is to discover what He already knows or to worry that we might miss His perfect plan. Our responsibility is to love Him, study His word, deepen our relationship with him—and learn to evaluate our choices in light of biblical wisdom. If we're doing these things, we can make our decisions in the confidence that we aren't somehow missing God's will."

God does know and already sees into the future and fully understands what you are going to be like as you mature and what would fulfill your life and who would fit well in where your life is going to go, the good and the bad. (I think we should change the wording of the wedding vows from "for better *or* worse" to "for better *and* worse" because both will come.) He knows this same "fulfilling life stuff" about your future sweet heart and He would like nothing more than to be asked by you to bring his wisdom to bear on the whole situation, especially in this area of relationships. Jesus said, "He would send a coun-selor" (God's Holy Spirit), one who would not only convict us of sin but lead us into all truth as well. I'm thinking this sounds like a plan to me. If He (God) knowing the future, knowing me better than I even know myself, and knowing what kind of person would be my soul mate—*and*—He would be willing to direct me and help me select a life's partner that would be right for both of us now, and in the future—bring it! Now that is an "arranged" marriage concept I can live with.

Bottom line, you can make whatever well intended commitment or vow of purity or whatever we may choose to call it—you can wear a ring or a necklace to help you remember your good intentions, but apart from the power of God's spirit dwelling within us and empowering us to walk with a pure heart before him, and our making a choice to listen to His prompting and claim His protection, we're toast. Did I just say don't wear the purity ring your parents gave you? No, I did not! I said the ring, apart from the power of the Holy Spirit living in your life, won't keep your heart pure. I'm also saying to grit your teeth and muscle your way through this relationship thing by discipline alone for however long it takes may make your heart chaste, it still will not make it pure.

Some of you will play with this and will even use the information we have given you in this material to your advantage, not so much to live in this area of relationships with integrity, but to manipulate and maneuver your way close to the fire, and to have some cute company when you get there. And you know what, you will think you have beaten the system. You may not become pregnant or get anyone else pregnant, and you probably won't catch anything serious, but you will have violated your conscience, and you will have defrauded the conscience of your partner(s). You will also have no knowledge of how you have impacted their life and their confidence before God, nor how Satan has used you to lift them to a rung on the biological ladder that they cannot safely occupy. Perhaps a rung from where he can destroy their witness or maybe even their life. I Peter 5:8 says, *"... Your enemy the devil prowls around like a roaring lion looking for someone to devour."* He is playing for keeps! He *does know* the truth and he too lives out his existence based on what he understands to be true {Life Lesson No.1}.

Your enemy also knows you are dangerous to him. You probably didn't even know that. If you allow the truth to set you free especially at the level of the heart where relationships happen, Satan knows he will lose a strategic battlefield in your life where he could usually take you out. He's taking out your friends with this every day and even your Christian friends and destroying their witness not only at school but at church and work too. He has already used some of *you* and your way of dealing with these issues to unravel the unity–and witness that could be there in your life.

If you don't think your life really makes all that much difference whether you walk close to the Lord, read Ezekiel 36:23 where God says *"… then the nations will know that I am the Lord, declares the Sovereign Lord, when I show myself holy **through you** before their eyes.* (Bold emphasis mine). Your life is a witness to what you believe, not because you are popular or occupy a position of leadership at school or at work, not because you are handsome or cute, but because God chose for your life and mine to bear witness of Him. And that simply put–is amazing!

God–*The God*–wants to show Himself holy through your and my life.

So much was that His intent that Jesus in Matthew Chapter 5 said it again in verses 13 through 16 that our lives are to be such that they actually "flavor" life all around us. He talked about us being like salt to the world and a light in the darkness. Verse 16 says our life can really be such a beacon that those who see our lives can recognize the activity of God there and glorify Him as a result. Wow!

My own personal, self-oriented, response when I first heard that was–well, good luck, God!

Then I had the privilege to hear a very respected friend by the name of Denny Holzbauer speak at our church one night on living a life that is holy and pleasing to the heart of God.

With his permission I have reconstructed some of what was shared that night in this next section. I want you to get the benefit of those thoughts, they are wise counsel.

God knowing and wanting to show Himself holy through us designed us, created us, and empowers us to be able to live life as it was originally intended, to live it "right"eously in fellowship with Him and thereby to live and be holy. (Don't bail on me yet, you should know me well enough by now that if this is beginning to sound "preachy" it is not where I am going with this. Keep reading.)

Therefore, I urge you, brothers, in view of God's mercy, to offer your bodies as living sacrifices, holy and pleasing to God—this is your spiritual act of worship. Do not be conformed any longer to the pattern of this world. But be transformed by the renewing of your mind

(It just keeps coming up how important it is
what we put into our minds and hearts?)

Romans 12: 1–2

It is God's will that you should be sanctified: that you should avoid sexual immorality; that each of you should learn to control his own body in a way that is holy and honorable, not in passionate lust like the heathen, who do not know God; and that in this matter no one should wrong his brother or take advantage of him. The Lord will punish men for all such sins, as we have already told you and warned you. For God did not call us to be impure, but to live a holy life. Therefore he who rejects this instruction does not reject men but God, who gives his Holy Spirit.

I Thessalonians 4:3–8

GOODBYE ABSTINENCE, HELLO HEART

94

> Therefore, prepare your minds for action; be self-controlled; set your
> hope fully on the grace to be given you when Jesus Christ is revealed.
> As obedient children, do not conform to the evil desires you had when
> you lived in ignorance. But just as he who called you is holy, so be
> holy in all you do, for it is written: Be holy, because I am holy.
> I Peter 1: 13–16

We are called to be holy as He is holy. Recognize the fact
that God's instruction in I Peter that you just read is not a
multiple choice directive. There are no A, B, C, or None of
the Above options offered. We are called to be and live Holy.
Why would He expect that, to demand that? I want to offer
the position because that is the way we were created to live,
and every other apparent option is a lesser life and often times
a total lie.

If you are truly a born again believer you have what is
referred to as "positional righteousness". That as we are in Jesus
Christ–God sees us through the sacrificed blood of His Son
and views us as holy. But that reference to a positional "holiness" is not what the preceding verses are calling us to. They are
calling us up to a practical living that is holy in every day life
kinda stuff. If we do not understand this expectation on our
lives to be what God has called us to we can easily abuse God's
grace by thinking it doesn't matter how we live or what we do
by saying we are in Christ, using as an excuse that God already
sees us as righteous.

But the righteous life has an enemy, and that enemy has a
very effective tool he uses against us. That tool, the No. 1 opponent to holiness is temptation. Denny defined temptation that
evening as being, "Anything that entices us to do that which
is wrong by promise of pleasure or gain." That definition has
stuck with me and keeps coming up right on target time after
time in my own life, and I believe it will in yours as well.

Now what you don't know about Ralph Dennis Holzbauer is that he has several world title kickboxing championships to his name. In the process of accomplishing these pretty impressive results he has learned how to go about studying his opponent and preparing for a fight. He knows how to identify their weaknesses, their strengths, their plan of attack. There are some things it will help you and I to know if we are going to have a chance in these battles with temptation. James, the brother of Jesus, gives us the "fight film" on this opponent, temptation.

First, understand that temptation is inevitable. You are going to be tempted! James says in Chapter 1 verse 13 not *if* you are tempted–*when* you are tempted. There is nowhere you can go where you will not be tempted. There is no island or special place that you could go to insure you would not be tempted. There is no magic or spiritual formula that you could memorize or gain any level of maturity where you would not be tempted. Temptation is inevitable.

Second, God has positively no part in temptation. James says in that verse that God, himself cannot be tempted and He tempts no one. He is Holy. For you or I to claim and use the excuse that God has brought this temptation into our lives and is enticing us to do that which violates His own heart with a promise of pleasure or gain is not only ridiculous–it is heresy.

Thirdly, sin is an individual matter, *"each one is tempted and carried away and enticed **by his own** lust,"* James continues NAS (bold type mine). There is no power, there is no pressure, including peer pressure (influence of your friends) that can force you to yield to that temptation and do things that are wrong. Sin occurs when we come into personal agreement with the temptation. "Yeah, I could get pleasure or gain from that." Nothing outside of your own choice causes you to sin and to take that temptation.

Fourth, sin is always something that will entice you. It will appeal to you, big time! Whatever form it takes, it will look incredibly good and be desirable to you. It has to be or you wouldn't be tempted. Here again the individuality of temptation shows up in that what tempts me that which might make me break out in a cold sweat trying to fight it, may seem silly to you. "You're tempted by that," you would chuckle? While at the same time something that would nauseate me would chew you up and spit you out because it has such an attraction to you. Pornography is one of those for me. Porn is not a problem for me—never has been. It isn't that I don't find the exposed female body incredibly beautiful and some of the interaction as enticing, it is that they take it too far. To the point of—well, gross! That doesn't mean it cannot be a huge struggle for the next person.

Temptation will always come to you through your thought processes. (Remember the "mind thing" and how very important it is what we allow into our minds?) Let's say you are walking along through your day and you see something or hear about some activity that looks good and appears to offer pleasure or gain to you. Perhaps it is a conversation about a party that went on last weekend. You hear that no parents were home and it makes you regret that you missed what went on—or a party that is going on tonight, and your mind races ahead to what "could" go on. Maybe it is simply that one of the doors to the ladies dressing room in a store at the mall isn't fully closed and you catch a glimpse in the reflection of a mirror of an attractive set of legs trying on some outfits. So you stop and spend more time at the clothing racks that are in a good position so you can "check it out." That is how temptation entices us. It comes to us through our eyes and ears, but it processes in our mind.

That word entice is often used as a fishing term. It describes what a fisherman uses "bait" for, to entice the response of the fish. It can also describe the pattern of our thought processes when something tempts us.

- First, the bait is dropped
- The inner desire is attracted to the bait (to this point it is only tempting)
- Sin occurs when we decide to check out the bait and we take it.
- (I loved the term that Denny used that night for how you can describe someone who decides to "check out the benefits of, and ultimately takes the bait". He said, "You call them Dead Fish!")
- Sin always results in tragic consequences.

I mentioned above that at the point at which the inner desire is being attracted to check out the bait, is still in the "temptation stage" but we have not yet committed ourselves, either in action or in the fantasy or our minds, to carrying out the desire that is being felt. That is why Steve Farrah in his book *Point Man* says, "Temptation is not sin, it is a call to battle!" Be reminded and encouraged that as humans, we live by choice. Now is when I get to make one–choice that is. Do I stay and watch the dressing room activity, or make plans to go to the party, or do I make a choice to as Paul said in I Corinthians 9:27, " ... *but I buffet my body and make it my slave* (rather than being a slave to it) *lest possibly, after having preached to others, I myself* (the message of my life) *should be disqualified?" NAS* (Added parenthesis emphasis mine.)

When God calls us to something, He always gives us the resources to accomplish that which He has called us to. One of the resources God gives us that helps us have a chance for handling temptation is a fruit of the Spirit called, Self Control. We cannot work it up on our own and be successful very long–it is a gift from God. And keep in mind here that the gifts of God, the wisdom and counsel of His Holy Spirit will not cheat you out of something good just for keeping the rules sake. It will be because it is right. Right for you, right for the situation, right for everyone involved or that could be involved–it will be right. You can depend on it.

Remember earlier when we talked about how one of the problems with our fantasies and "playing" with things in our minds is that the fantasy story line never has any consequences. Remember, we always win. The fantasy plays out in our mind like we envision it.

How do we know that if we play out a sexual fantasy in our mind, or secretly in actual life, a choice that dishonors both ourselves and our Creator, that it won't turn out okay? Because, *"the wages of sin is death"(Romans 6:23)!*

Sin always has tragic consequences.

It has proven helpful on more than one occasion when I become aware of myself playing with how desirable something seems to be or how I might gain from its fulfillment is to remind myself that the final pain will soon erase the temporary pleasure of my sin. Is there pleasure in sin–don't ask foolish questions. Hebrews 11:25 says there is pleasure in sin, but that it is short lived.

When the Holy Spirit sets off the alarm signal in you that you are being tempted–you can ignore it and resist His voice. Remember, we are creatures that live by choice. When we ignore God's voice, we begin to have a more and more difficult time hearing God's prompting. And when you do ignore His counsel, you heat up the desire to satisfy your own flesh. Satan then intervenes and he fills us not so much with hatred for God as forgetfulness of God. And he pours water on our passion to live a holy life.

You see, we don't just need, we are desperate for God's Holy Spirit to fill us and empower us to walk in fullness of life. To keep us mindful of a bigger story than "who is going to make me feel good—about me." To enable us to live our lives *with* great desire and passion for all of life.

Will that set us up for probable frustration? Yes!

God set this world up, after the choices and subsequent "fall" of Adam and Eve, so that it doesn't work. What? You heard it right. God guarantees this world, this life, as we know it—does not, will not, cannot work. He has no intention of allowing us to be fully satisfied in a fallen life style. In Genesis 3, after Adam and Eve have made their choice (that human thing again) and disobeyed God and eaten of the fruit of the tree of the knowledge of good and evil, He takes them out of the garden and places a guard at the gate–why? I always looked at it as punishment, I mean they are being banished from the garden. And make no mistake it was a huge loss for them. It demonstrated the brokenness of their relationship with God and the real actual death to their life–not existence–life. But it was not just for discipline only that they were removed from the garden and a guard placed at the gate–it was also for their protection, so they could not reenter the garden and eat of the tree of life that was also in the middle of the garden and remain in their fallen state forever. He had not written them off, he doesn't write you off.

God didn't forget how to create after He had a day of rest. He could have solved the whole Adam and Eve problem real easy you know. I would have squashed them and made two more. Why didn't He–why doesn't He squash you and me? There are plenty more out there where we came from.

Because His heart toward Adam and Eve–and His heart toward you is Good!

His commitment is for all eternity, not only as long as you keep the rules, or as long as you don't mess up too bad. Oh, He is God, and He is holy and righteous and just. And He does not turn his head and ignore our sin. His love just made a way for paying the penalty for those choices against His heart.

In fact the real question for your whole life, yes even the questions about "*Do I have what it takes*" and "*Am I captivating to you*"—the question that every other question rests upon is:

> What is God's heart toward you?
>
> Who are you because of who He made you to be?

At the very deepest part of those questions is the desire for value and worth, a search for love. Remember Chesterton's observation that a man is really seeking God even when he is knocking on the door of a house of prostitution? Can you now begin to see the heart desire behind his knocking? Is he looking for sex? At the physical level, yes, but here the sex is an attempt to satisfy the need of the heart for being wanted, accepted, loved–even if he has to pay for it!

And so God did–pay for it. Once and for all at all of the brothels where you take your heart looking for acceptance, and value, and love. Read John 3:16. I know many of you have heard that section of scripture so many times you no longer "hear it". Go back and read it again, but try to see it for the first time—at the level of the heart of God.

What is God's heart toward you? It is *the* question Satan asked of Eve in the garden. He didn't ask Eve if she had ever tried the fruit before, from a fruit tasting perspective. He is challenging–and encouraging Eve to challenge the very heart of God. "He is holding out on you, he says, He doesn't want you to eat from that tree because He (God) knows that the day you do, you will be like Him."

It is the real question you are asking when you fear you might be missing out on the fun if you follow God's principles and guidelines for life and try living out some of the sugges-tions in this book. It is the hidden heart behind the question you are asking each other when you want someone to "validate' your feminine desirability or your manliness by their response to you.

If I am totally honest with this whole issue of God's heart toward me, especially in this arena called romance, I am mostly concerned that I might miss the party and all the fun, only to find out later it didn't make any real difference anyway.

"We are not necessarily doubting that God will do the best for us; we are wondering how painful the best will be."   C. S. Lewis

---

Seven

Dive, Dive, Dive!

Let's go deeper than gut level.

Some of you have already crossed the lines and you know there is no way back; you can't be "physically virgin" again. You believe this message is not for you because it can't save you from failing in this area. There may be a few that have stepped across the line and you don't know for sure if you want to cross back over even if you could–I mean it is fun and gains you a certain level of acceptance, and, why fight it anyway?

It is also likely that some of you were taken "across the line" against your will. I'm told that the average for girls between the ages of 6 and 18 is that 1 in every 3 or 4 girls have been abused before they reach adulthood, and the average for guys is not very much better. The guy's number may even be higher than the girl's but we guys think we can't ask for help or we'll appear weak, or we're too ashamed, so it often stays unreported. So in a group of just the guys and gals you know, there is a good chance that some have been hurt in some incredible ways that no one but that person and their heavenly Father could ever know. And, if that "someone" happens to not be just someone you know, but was and is you, I don't want to be casual with your pain. Without going into a lengthy discussion, if you have been used or abused, you need to know that is was not your fault. It was not your fault!

Hear it again. It was not your fault! And rest in the fact that you can be in a safer place and you can respond now in ways you may not have been able to respond before. Also realize as long as it is kept a secret, the hurt will never begin to heal. In fact keeping it a secret only gives power to the evil side of what happened. The statement that time heals all things–is a lie. Time does help with some things, but not with the deep wounds of our hearts. So no matter how long ago it might have been–or if it is still happening now, go to your Pastor or Youth Pastor or a truly trusted family member (one that you know from experience will go to bat with you) and share what is or has gone on and get some help in this battle. It is time!

There are some of you reading this that look good and smell good and go to church and sing in the choir and maybe you even make good grades or are a great team player at work–and yet you feel filthy and trashy on the inside because you play with this relationship thing. Maybe in your mind or maybe on the internet or watching adult movies. Maybe with books and magazines and nobody knows it but you. But you know it–and your heavenly Father knows it. And you are just sure if you ever admitted your struggles in this area, why you would rather die first than embarrass your family and friends. And you know God could never forgive you. Maybe you have even tried to stop or change and you can't give it up. It is never too late. The struggle is never too big. And the victory is oh so worth the fight! Do the most courageous thing that can be done in this situation—step up and ask for help.

There very possibly are also some of you here who don't know why, but you don't orient your thoughts in relationships the same way we've been discussing. And you aren't sure where you fit in God's plans, if at all. The homosexual world is a painful world and one most of us aren't good at understanding the why's and why not's of. Don't let Satan lie to you and convince you the truths presented in these pages are not for you. We all have the same needs for acceptance and validation. Scripture talks about a friend who is closer than a brother and the relationship that Jonathan and David had that was closer than a man and a woman. Don't misinterpret what that means. There is a level of emotional intimacy that two men can share or two women can share that can be incredibly understanding, and free and personal and truly intimate, in ways that even a husband and wife might find insensitive with its openness and blunt honesty–but it is not sexual. Stay with me.

Know this: you are not broken goods. To believe that you cannot live with victory in the areas you are struggling with is a lie of your enemy, the devil, and not the heart of your heavenly Father toward you. Whether you chose to go too far in your physical relationships or were taken there by others, "you are His child and in His eyes you have always been an innocent and beautiful daughter or son." He can restore your pure heart and prepare you for relationships that may well be beyond your wildest dreams.

Now I want every eye right here (think about that statement for a minute–where else could you be looking and read this sentence?)

No matter where you find yourself, you are reading this for a reason, and that reason is bigger than you could ever have imagined. Some of you may be reading this in a small discussion group and truth be known you come to just hang out with your buds. Some of you came to this book looking for hope that you haven't totally blown it forever. Some of you hope to find some help in keeping your heart *from* blowing it.

But God has a higher agenda here than making you pure physically or even attempting to keep you that way. (Did I say that out loud?)

> *God has a higher agenda here than making you pure*
> *physically or even attempting to keep you that way.*

He wants you to come alive, really alive in Him. To be all He created you to be. To live large in His huge story of redemption and love. He wants you to be Christ-like thereby reflecting His image in the very way you live out your life. There are people in your world that will listen and help you begin to see the truth in these areas. And you can begin to live in the light of those truths.

Many of us who are farther down life's road than you may be at this time are still figuring it out too as God leads our lives into a fresh understanding of His heart toward us and how hard it is to attempt to live life by rules and guidelines, even good ones, with no heart behind them.

Let us help.

There are very likely also some of you who are clueless about this relationship thing with God through His Son, Jesus Christ. Remember Life Concept No. 2? The things I believe about God do not change the truth about God at all. You need to know that no matter what you think about church or Christianity, you will give an account for your life before God because He says you will, just like everyone will. To toss aside the truths God has given you and ignore his commands is an indication that you think you can handle His wrath. If you believe that you will live your life based on it, but you will die a fool. If that sounds hard and unkind, you still don't understand the path Jesus chose to walk to buy back our choice for freedom from sin and death.

There are some things in this life worth fighting for. Your

heart and what you are willing to give it away to is one of them!

Eight

The Loose Ends

I made a promise in the very beginning of this book to bounce around a couple of ideas with you that we haven't really tackled yet but are very much worth brainstorming together.

In specific they were:

Will there be anything like sex in heaven?

If I said, "I believe there will be", would it get your attention, make you wonder?

Ladies,

Imagine being in a relationship with a lover where you are fully known at the very deepest secret parts of all that you are, nothing to have to hide or be ashamed of—no secrets, none. And still know that you are fully accepted. That your lover looks at you and sees beauty, not fixed up, surface beauty, but beauty at the heart and core of your very being, as well as how your look–and he is captured by it. Imagine in the intimacy of this relationship that you are valued beyond any level of worth, and loved without limits. That the one in whose eyes you find your reflection would give anything–and everything, to express his love for you. That his strength, his influence, all that he is, is for your protection and enjoyment. That you are his, and he is yours. You could, and you would want to give yourself away to this person in worshipful, passionate love.

Guys,

Imagine a relationship where your value is never questioned. Where your fears are erased and your wildest imaginations of true intimacy are real. Where you can give yourself–all that you are, with nothing held back, because you are already fully and totally known and loved. Loved for who you are, not for what you can do or act like you can do. Having nothing to prove, you also could give yourself away, perhaps for the first time ever in worshipful adoration of this one that you love. You would not need to give even a thought for yourself and be focused only in expressing your love to another because you are so already loved.

Is this just an unrealistic fantasy or could it be an accurate description of our relationship with our creator in eternity?

> Known
> Forgiven
> Restored
> Loved
> Alive!

Then perhaps the real question is not "will there be sex in heaven"? Maybe, just maybe, sex is an image, a reflection of something else. And the better question might be, "will there be worship in heaven?" Because if I could find myself in the confidence of that imaginary relationship we described, but here on earth with no "me" needs to attempt to satisfy, or fears of not satisfying and measuring up. Fully known and fully loved. I believe I could give myself away to my bride in a very real way in the intimacy of romance, and for those brief moments in time actually *worship* her as the object of my love. And she me.

Ladies and Gentlemen, it doesn't get any better than that!

And that **is** our forever relationship with the God who loves us and pursues us with a passion we can only imagine. Every one of you have been given a proposal of marriage, by a king– THE KING. The guests have been invited, the table is set, the feast is being prepared–don't miss that party for anything!

You let this play out in your own mind as it seems right to you, for these are the thoughts of a man who has had a beautiful relationship here on this earth, but who also knows the fears of acceptance and hesitancies of "performance" that two lovers hold secret even in the best this world can offer.

What is true intimacy?

You already know for yourself, but I think of it as being fully known. All of your strengths. All of your weaknesses. All of everything—and fully loved. And then offering that knowing, accepting love to someone else.

What does it make me feel to be physically and emotionally close? How close is too close?

Good question. I thought you would never ask. Remember the biological hand grenade ladder? Just like alcohol and drugs and chocolate we all come with differing dispositions or abilities to handle certain levels of things. A level of physical closeness that you can handle as no big deal might take me off the charts. (Be careful though, it is possible that your ability to handle a certain level of physical activity with someone else may be from familiarity rather than emotional separation. Sort of a "been there, done that, no big deal anymore type of thing.")

Can some people get "closer" than others without getting in trouble? Is it okay for Christian couples to make out? How far should Christian's go, physically, in their dating interactions?

This is a great question. Believe it or not, I asked this same question myself of a group of twenty-ish year old single adults on a camping trip one night around a campfire. I asked them, "Is it okay for Christians to make out?" These were sharp, attractive, intelligent, single adults, with a variety of perspectives on God and life and each other. The conversation went around the fire several times discussing the pros and cons of a really good "smooch" session. Especially on a cool night like it was that night with the fire sparkling on tan faces and reflecting in beautiful eyes, and sweatshirts and sleeping bags feeling all snuggly. And inside my head I was shouting, "What were you thinking? What possessed you to bring up this subject with this group of young adults, out in the woods, hormones off the charts, on a campout with me, the lame brain one, and the only married sponsor (chaperon, warden, whatever)."

As the discussion continued, the group moved more from how much fun it is to what about the other person–the one you are kissing. How do you know what you are saying to them at a deeper level? You don't know how they are thinking about themselves and how needy they may feel. You think you can handle it, but you won't know for sure until *after* you're done. The problem as they saw it was that both "kissers" might not be on the same page of what it was meaning to them and what they read into it. By the time it was over, it was too late to back up and un-send the message or undo the potential damage. This group of class young adults decided without my intervention (believe it or not I was only a witness to this conversation–once started, I did not participate), that out of sensitivity for each other, until you knew and understood where you each were in the relationship (at whatever level of commitment) and could be confident that the messages these kisses were sending were falling on understanding and healthy lips and hearts; it was the better path to *not* **kiss.**

I was blown away. I honestly don't know if I would have been mature enough to help take the conversation in that direction if I had been one of the single guys (especially with the particular group of ladies that were gathered around that campfire) but it was more than a little eye-opening to hear the other guys and the girls express their hearts so openly and vulnerably with each other. (Some of whom did not know each other at all two days earlier when we embarked on this outing.)

You have already noticed I didn't give you an answer on should Christians make out or how far can they go in their physical interactions with each other in their dating relationships? I invited you instead to hear the perspective of some very personable and open young adults, much like yourself, with all of the same desires for closeness and intimacy and response hard wired into their hearts that you have, and benefit from their thoughts. Now you decide, for you, where you would sit in this circle. You get to benefit from reading their thoughts— you get to live with yours.

Is it different (that whole physical, touchy-feely, warm, hot, closeness thing for Christians than for those not professing a belief structure? If so, why and how is it different in our responsibility to each other?

It doesn't have to be different with people who do not profess a spiritual belief structure in their lives. Truth and caring and sensitivity can be expressed by anyone willing to set their own agenda aside and consider the other person. Remember the "inside out" way of thinking mentioned in the first chapter that can come into play when we have a Christ-centered heart? No better example of how it might be played out than in the way we interact physically with each other. How much does one person concern himself / herself with the impact of their actions on the other person? Am I a giver of my strength to this relationship or am I a consumer for my needs?

At what point do you lose your virginity? Are the standards the same for Christians and non-believers?

This one is pretty deep, but I also promised you we would go straight at the issues—even the tough ones.

Remember that the whole umbrella this book falls under is not just *Goodbye Abstinence* but...

Hello Heart!

Think again on Life Concept No. 3

LIFE CONCEPT No. 3

ALL OF THE CRUCIAL ISSUES OF LIFE
COME FROM THE HEART—
guard it above all else.

*Proverbs 4:23 says, "above all else
guard your heart for it is
the wellspring of life."*

You've heard it all your life without noticing it, but we acknowledge with little clichés the very truth defined in Proverbs 4:23. Statements like:

"Come on–put your heart into it".

"He just doesn't have the heart for it."

"I love you with all my heart"

You could come up with numerous other "heart" oriented phrases without really having to think too hard. However, the question on your mind right now could logically be, what does the heart have to do with the question, "At what point does a person lose their virginity?"

Go with me.

There is a really interesting story in I Samuel 16:7. God has sent Samuel, His prophet to the home of Jesse to select a man. A man God says is to follow Saul as the next King of Israel. Saul has been casual with God's instructions for him and Samuel has informed Saul that his casualness with God's instructions is the same as being disobedient. As a result, God has said, "I will replace Saul with another king." Jesse brings his sons in one at a time for Samuel to meet. As would be the custom in those days, Jesse brings in his sons introducing first the oldest and then progresses toward the youngest. Now Samuel is trying to evaluate each of Jesse's sons for the right clue to which one God has chosen to be king. Even Samuel is having trouble knowing how to judge which of the young men will be the best king. They each look so strong and capable in Samuel's eyes:

"But the Lord said to Samuel, "Do not consider his appearance or his height, for I have rejected him. The LORD does not look at the things man looks at. Man looks at the outward appearance, but the LORD looks at the heart."
(I Samuel 16:7)

So God is saying right out loud that He looks at issues and life different than we as typical humans do. You haven't read this far in this book not to have that figured out by now.

Jeremiah 17:10 says what God is looking at/for when He looks at our heart.

Jeremiah 17:10, "I the LORD search the heart and examine the mind, to reward a man according to his conduct, according to what his deeds deserve."

He is looking at our motive, the why of our actions. You may also remember that our actions are simply a belated announcement of what we have already purposed in our hearts to do as they are released through our thoughts (our mind).

Matthew 5:28, "But I tell you that anyone who looks at a woman lustfully has already committed adultery with her in his **heart**."

Let's go to the author of purity and chasteness and who sets the standards for all of life. From God's perspective, you tell me, when does a person lose their virginity? Is it when they undress and climb in the sack, or is it when they agree in their hearts to undress and climb in?

Ladies, your parents and your gynecologist will never know you have been "sleeping around" in the fantasies of your mind because there will be no physical evidence of a compromised physical virginity. And guys, we don't carry the same physical evidences of having played with sex as the ladies do, even if we not only played in our minds but have been actually acting out as the lover boy. So it is possible neither of you will ever be exposed—except in your hearts before God.

This may seem hard to you, but who has not fallen in their thoughts? No one. And I do not stand above you in this issue, but alongside you. We are actually just living proof of Romans 3:23, *"...for all have sinned and fall short of the glory of God,"* and Romans 3:10, *"There is no one righteous not even one ... "* or Isaiah 53:6, *"We all like sheep have gone astray, each one of us has turned to his own way; and the Lord has laid on Him the iniquity of us all."*

We *all* have need of a Savior who can restore our purity.

At what point do you lose your virginity–ask your heart.

Recreational sex–what's up with that?

If it were legit–I would choose it over tennis any day!

I think I need more of your input on this one. Would you agree that you can take almost anything, anything, and treat it like recreation? One person fishes and hunts to feed his family. That being true, those could be labeled as necessary activities. Another person joins the local bass club or deer camp and the same activity that was somewhat of a necessity for one person, becomes the hobby for another. It is recreation to him. One person rides a bicycle as her only source of transportation to get to school or work, another races for trophies on weekends. Almost anything can be treated with a recreational mindset. Does the fun go out of sex if you treat the activity, or the person you are with, with casualness; or if your real motive is to gather physical conquest "trophies" to put on the shelf in your room?

I'm not meaning to be callously blunt with this. It is not hard to understand that anything that can offer such physical pleasure as sex and the associated responses of a partner you are attracted to would be incredibly tempting to just enjoy anytime and almost anywhere the opportunity offered itself.

"But doesn't the Bible says it is sin to do that? If it is so *bad* how can it still be so fun?" The Bible also says there is pleasure in sin (Hebrews 11:25). How about this one? Proverbs 9:17 says, *"Stolen water is sweet and food eaten in secret is delicious."* If you understand that verse then you can understand why playing footsy with your buddy's girl friend while he is all wrapped up in the movie would feel off the charts, or flirting with your roommates boyfriend–because of the response factor involved. (Even if you are not particularly interested in her or him to date, the response to you feels very nice. That can be attributed in part to the competitive nature of us as guys. For just that few moments you are "one up" on the other guy, his girl would just as soon be with you.) Do you think for a moment God doesn't know how He wired us? He knows the passion and desire He placed within you. He knows what it was put there for. And He knows very well the many ways you and I can attempt to satisfy those longings.

The problem comes in that somehow in His (God's) economy of life, there is a depth of soul emotion (the inner you and me) that enters into the physical activity of sex that takes it out of the realm of simple recreation. Somehow it is attached to something deeper in our hearts that says it is more. It is how shall I say it–"sacred"? It is set apart for a coming together of a man and a woman to experience each other in a way that has more meaning than a game of cards or bowling.

What about the couples thing?

I know this isn't necessarily about abstinence or sex, but in many ways it is about the spirit of relationships and their impact on each other. Maybe I should ask you first: How does it affect your youth group or your fellowship of friends when couples begin to form and date within the group?

Is it no big deal? Does it separate the fellowship of the group? Does it even matter at all?

My personal experience is that it is very unusual for a group of friends to continue to hang out well together when couples begin to form within the group. The new relationships are usually very consuming of the couples attention and time. There can be risk of jealousy if members of the "group" give too much attention to either partner of the new couple (sometimes nothing actually different than the way you were interacting before, but now it seems to take on a different meaning, potentially). This is not always the case nor does it have to be, but it seems to be the norm. I have seen couples handle themselves so cool in the group interaction that the fellowship rocks right on as before, but that is the exception. Then you have the potential of the couple having an argument or breaking up and what do you do with that–as a group? It will seem as if the members of the group are "taking sides" with one partner or the other, and there is no way to walk down the middle of the road in these arguments without getting "run over" at some point.

Bottom line, it can happen and work okay–but probably some rocky roads to navigate in the process.

Where from Here?

I want to give you some practical steps to help put reality to this. This is not the "how to" section of the book; don't memorize these as tips and techniques. These are some suggestions that have proven true and helpful in my own life and in the lives of numerous others I have had the privilege to know and learn from.

First: Know that this is not something you will be able to be casual with. You must guard your heart! (And you know by know when I use the term "heart" I am not referring to the blood pumping muscle in your chest. I am describing the deepest part of you—the total of your mind, emotions, and spirit, the real **you**.) I don't think I can say it too much, what you allow into your mind will have a tremendous impact upon your success and the consistency of your walk through this relationship thing. Regardless of your good intentions, you will not be successful if you watch/read/listen to/focus on the things that set your emotions on fire. If I place no limits on my thoughts, if I play with them and don't take them captive when they want to run off in every imaginable direction, I will really struggle with everything we've talked about.

Do you mean I can't go to certain movies or listen to some

of my music or have to be careful what I watch on TV? "Come on, how far do I have to go with this?"

Only as far as you want to have victory in this area of your life and are willing to guard your heart. You go before the Lord and ask Him when and where you are submitting yourself to the things that do not honor Him, or you. Ask Him when you are "sampling the waters" and if you will be honest with yourself, most of you will want to make some changes in how you entertain your mind.

Think about it, the group you hang out with asks you if you want to go see a movie and you say, "I would enjoy hanging out with you guys, but God is showing me how important it is to really guard my heart, and I know where my thoughts can run if I'm not careful. Maybe another time." They might say out loud to you, or to your other friends, "Boy, is he/ she weird." But you would also hold a level of respect with them as someone who lives by their convictions and God might just use that salty light to impact their lives.

Second: Avoid the very opportunity for failure. As I am writing this very paragraph I am in my study/office (that used to be our dining room) and I am at home alone. There is no one here to see what I am doing. What I want to do right now is drink a Mountain Dew. I like Mountain Dew. I may even borderline love Mountain Dew. My resolve to not drink any more Mountain Dew is because I am attempting to get my lazy carcass into better physical shape. And I know from experience that when I drink carbonated drinks and then try to run, it adds to a condition often referred to as "sucking wind". It affects my lung's capability to accept and process oxygen. I know this. I have experienced it before. It won't be any different this time. And when I am running in a little while, I will promise myself *never* to drink another Mountain Dew. But the truth of the matter is that my resolve to be wise in this "tempta-tion" and not drink one right now, is made easier not so much by my discipline or my knowledge of the consequences, or fear of getting caught, but because we are out of Mountain Dew. There isn't any more in the refrigerator.

There are times when simply avoiding the opportunity to fail is the wise choice.

You will not be successful tempting yourself with tan-talizing situations and settings and hope you can walk away unburned. Bottom line, you go out on a date with Mr. or Miss Hottie and drive out on Kisse Poo Lane and think you are going to stay cool. You might come away once, maybe even twice, maybe a hundred times, but keep playing and you will stumble. Or, you make the choice, up front, not to subject yourself and your date to the temptation to push the limits, by where you go and what you do. When my flesh and its desires are viewed as one of the options, and not as a battle, I can begin to weigh the options and the perceived benefits. And some-times they look really good. (I believe *enticing* is the operative word here, remember James 1:13–15?) The apparent options can look good enough to make me give it a taste before I am even willing to consider the consequences.

Now, with that whole concept in mind, put your hands out where I can see them, and back slowly away from the Mountain Dew, and you will be okay.

Third: Flee! There are just some situations where your best efforts to avoid the chance of temptation or to minimize the opportunity all together simply are not enough. You can look up and find yourself right where you said you didn't want to be (but right where you "wanted to be", if you know what I mean). The only path of protecting yourself and your date from sure disaster is to Flee. Run! Hook um up! Hit the road

Jack! Get out of Dodge! This may seem like a weakling or less than admirable approach. A real person of character would stand up to this situation and politely say, "No, but thanks for asking," to this incredible creature God made and is now placed before you.

Hello here!

God knew our makeup when He instructed Paul to write in 2nd Timothy to flee youthful lusts. And "youthful" doesn't refer to the timeframe or age bracket outside of which lustful thoughts and responses are no longer an issue. It's just the timeframe when they start. Here me on this–it doesn't go away with the number of birthdays you have had. And when He said, "Flee", He didn't mean hold hands and pray about it. He meant what He said. He knows us–He knows *you*. Flee!

Fourthly: Right now this concept of living from our hearts and being sensitive to what our desires are really asking of us, the things we have been sharing together in this book and talking about will seem so right to you, they do to me too. In two weeks, or maybe two days, it will not seem so clear, and may even become hazy enough as to really not seem to apply at all. What we have been talking about is incredibly simple–not easy.

Simple.

But the biggest stumbling block you will face from this will not be from your enemy the devil. He is all about his agenda, no doubt, but the easiest way for this to fade in its effectiveness in your life will be for you to think you will remember what God has said to you through this. In Hebrews, God cautions several times, ". .don't drift—do not forget." Deut. 4:9, *"Only be careful and watch yourselves closely so that you do not forget the things your eyes have seen or let them slip from your heart as long as you live."* You see, this process of walking in relationship with God through the revelation and power of His Spirit is the way He chooses for us to walk with Him through all the arenas of our lives. So we're not just gaining wisdom for this area of physical responses and relationships thing only. In fact the second part of the verse in Deuteronomy 4 instructs us that not only is this for our lives today, but we are to *"teach them* (the truths we have seen and learned) *to your children and to their children after them."* (Parenthesis mine)

Therefore, I don't think I can encourage you enough to keep a journal, your walk with God. Not a diary of "today I went to the dentist". Do that if you want to, but I'm talking about a record of God's hand in your life. God's word is holy and good for instruction, and we should spend time in his presence there. But at 2:00 a.m., when you feel as though your life is coming unraveled, it is difficult, for me at least, sometimes to gain much comfort from what God did in the lives of Paul or Peter, or anybody for that matter, 2000 years ago. However, on numerous occasions when I have re-read what God spoke into John's life, this John, I have been encouraged to continue in faith, to remember His faithfulness, and be reminded that this day or this event is a piece of a much larger story. This current struggle, or victory, is not the whole story for my life–or yours. When I am reminded, when I remember, I am encouraged to stand again and fight the battle of faith, and know that what He has done he will continue to do. That He began this work of Christ-likeness in my life, and yours, and He has committed to complete it. Hallelujah! Bring it!

Finally, one of the greatest helps in this area of the heart for me and I want to suggest it will be for you as well, is to join together with a couple of other guys if you are a guy and girls if you are a girl and meet on a regular basis to encourage each other, to share your struggles and enjoy your victories.

The details of some suggested how to's for this type of small group are defined well in other books, but it is an incredible influence to have a band of brothers or sisters to walk together with through life's battles. (I have also found it very helpful to have a variety of ages in the group with varying spiritual maturity levels in this band of pilgrims you involve yourself with, but that one is up to you.)

Did God purposefully give us a desire for intimacy and then plant impossible obstacles in the way of satisfying it? NO! That would violate His own guidelines when he says *"Fathers, do not exasperate your children, that they may not lose heart.",* *(Colossians 3:21* NAS*)* and He can't do that. The one thing God cannot do is violate his own rightness. God gave each of us a desire for intimacy because that is what He wants for each of us. First with Him, and then with each other.

There **is** a beautiful relationship waiting for you, each of you. Husband / Wife? I don't know. For most of you, yes. For some perhaps not in that way. Perhaps God has given you a heart that is His alone, and you need to know you will never feel cheated in this.

Again, you also must know and live in the light of our inability, impossibility, to walk this path, successfully without His help. Romans 8:26 says *"In the same way, the Spirit helps us in our weakness…"*

There you have it. We **can** let our hearts live with desire and agree that intimacy is what we do want, because we were created for such, and we can seek God for his ways to satisfy that longing within us. He did not plant those seeds deep in our heart of hearts without also providing a God-honoring way to fulfill them. Will you feel the frustration of a world that doesn't work this side of heaven–absolutely! But we can live in the truth, not the lie, and it will be good.

I make the following statement in some of the arenas I am privileged to speak that, "The wonderful thing I find about most of the young men and women I get to meet and spend time around, whether they are in Junior High, High School, College or even into young adulthood is that they do want truth. Truth. Not partial truth, because someone thinks you are not able to handle it. The real stuff. The real, honest to goodness, no holes barred, truth."

The qualifying observation in my own life to that honestly stated compliment about you, the reader, is that young people, while you are certainly truth seekers, you are not always truth responders.

Knowing the truth. Knowing the good path is a major part of the equation. The rest is your call. You live by choice. You see truth is not just a series of correct facts or data–truth is a person. "*I am the* **truth** *the way and the life, no one comes to the Father except thru me" (John 14:6).* (Bold emphasis added)

That truth, the person and a relationship with Jesus Christ can and will set us free!

Safe? No way.

Easy? Some of the time, but other times a battle of life and death proportions! Will the battle get nasty and will there be casualties? Guaranteed.

Will you ever doubt even the truth? My life experience says you will. I call it refining fire! The toughest part of living a life of faith is learning to live *as the person God says you are.* What is thought about you on earth is not nearly as significant as what is known about you in heaven.

And this is what God knows about you, and reflects His heart toward you ...

The Lord your God is with you He is mighty to save,
He takes great delight in you
He rejoices over you with singing
He will quiet you with His love
Zephaniah 3:17

Walk well–like the children of the great King!

Epilogue

Parents' Chalk Talk

The picture you are painting...

Whether you realized you were choosing the job or not, Moms, Dads, when you became a parent, one of the many job descriptions you signed on to fill, and one which you must accept is the opportunity, and the responsibility of helping your children identify areas they are gifted in. Every person has strengths, and yes we all have weaknesses as well; it balances us somewhat. Your adventure is to help them find those strengths that are God-given, for who they are. Quite a commitment here, but it is you, Dad, who bestows the strength and power to their lives, both sons and daughters. Mom, you balance us guys with your nurturing and care giving and mercy. But Dad, you are the primary one to show the sons how to be a man, and you show the daughters how she should expect to be treated by one. We're talking about their hearts here.

Once you feel you have begun to identify some areas of strength, help them find ways they can apply those gifts. Perhaps arenas in the family or at school or church. They need to experience some areas where they can be successful. Not necessarily areas where you were successful, or would like to have been. Help identify places and areas where *they* can be successful. Where your children can gain a sense of "weightiness" for who they are. It may be that they are extremely sensitive to details, or great encouragers to other kids. Maybe they are courageous and just will not be intimidated very easily by problems or people. Perhaps they are quick or fast in their motor skills or can remember a series of instructions well. For example, Rebekah, our youngest daughter, has always had a better grasp for the conceptualizing of things more than her peer group at any given age would typically have (probably got it from my side of the family). When she was very young and playing soccer, the coaches would have the kids practice dribbling the ball through a series of cones in the middle of the field. Most of the kids saw it as "how fun, to weave through the little orange cones." Rebekah seemed to understand from the beginning that the cones represented the opposing players and the exercise was to dribble the ball through them to score. So why did she choose to play defense where she would only kick the ball once to head it back down the field the other way, God alone has that answer. (Probably got that from Jean's side of the family.)

Your only other choice, Mom, Dad, is to leave them searching. And they will search for who they are and what gives their life value, until they find someone they think can give them their answers. Now you tell me, if you are not going to be involved here, in the world we offer them today, where do *you* suggest they begin looking?

Moms, your roll here is every bit as critical. It is you who gives the stabilizing early years. The years psychologists say form our very personalities and character traits for the rest of our lives. In many ways, thank goodness you are the primary influencer during that formative time. If we tried to do it alone, just us guys, without your balance, we might all be wandering around like Tarzan in loin cloths. You, Mom, are the one who makes life fun and worth fighting for. Believe it or not, you lay the foundation for everything else. Yes, of course, you too can help your kids identify the areas of strength in their lives and initiate ways or support ways where they can "invest" those talents and grow. And you must team together with your husband in this process.

Most kids have not really bought into or have settled on what they personally believe through their teen years. Their convictions about truth and life simply aren't defined and solidified yet. They are beginning to process it without even realizing it, but their thoughts have not yet been challenged by some of the options life holds out to them. If you "check out" of their lives because they are 14 or 17 and because they don't seem to listen anymore; or if you feel "they get all they need" from their involvement in the youth group at church or because they haven't been in any trouble, then you vacate the seat in the coaching and cheering section for their lives that God intended for *you* to occupy. They are still very much open to pressures from their friends or people they wish were their friends. Most kids, yours included, are desperately trying to fit in and not stick out. You can lose them before you realize they are changing, and they are masters at playing double rolls. You were. I was. Most of you know exactly what I mean when I say it is possible to be one person when you are at home, and be a very different person when you are with friends or away from home. We are almost not recognizable as the same person. Kids can play church and good kid on Sunday and be the foulest mouthed, drink it up, act it out kids the rest of the week.

You must stay plugged in!

And, Mom, when it comes to your sons, it is crucial at

the appropriate time to release them to Dad, emotionally, to initiate them into being a man. For your daughters, Mom, you help paint the picture they should expect to see in a man, what he looks like and what is important in him. Help her understand there is a difference when a guy comes to her *looking* to validate his strength (the "tell me I'm okay–let me prove that I have what it takes," kind of a guy) and when she meets a young man who *offers* her his strength. No one knows better than you ladies that there is a major difference between the two. (If you haven't read the whole book you might want to look in Chapter 5 for the specifics of what we are referring to here.)

Some of you are saying to yourself, "Great!" the *Dad* walked out of my children's lives a long time ago (or maybe he is walking out right now). Perhaps it was the *Mom* who checked out to go find a life that would mean more for her. That might prompt someone to say, "Okay Mr. Answer Person, what do I do now and how do I balance the influence needed in my son's or daughter's life?" I wish I had an easy fix for you. But know that your children have the Lord, and He knows what they need. He may use an extended family member or a member of your church, perhaps a Youth Pastor or Sunday School teacher or a teacher or coach at school to influence your child. Know that all is not lost. You will just have to be sensitive to the need for balancing of influence in their life and not try to do it all yourself–because you can't! You cannot.

And that "good" news should change the intensity of your prayer life!

Now let me address an area that we can be feeling really good about and all the while be really blowing it for our kids. As parents, we can unknowingly set an atmosphere or image before our children that literally strangles their willingness to be open with their struggles and be willing to come to us and be vulnerable to seek the very help and input they need from us. For whatever reasons, we as adults and parents like to present the image that we somewhat have our act together. I do, you do. We struggle to think that our kids and those we influence may not want to follow us if they see us struggling and stumbling in our own lives. I have to learn to allow my family to point out blind spots and give them permission to disagree with me, in a respectful way, and confess that I may not always get it exactly right the first time–or the 31ˢᵗ time. Can you believe that? That I, the Dad, or you, the Mom, might still be learning things too as life progresses. Amazing!

If I always have the right answer. If I never accept their way, or their process of handling things for their life, as a possible path, then they either begin to try to live life my way, to be pleasing to me, or they reject me completely and pay only token gesture respect to me just to not rock the boat. That all can happen while they are living in contempt of my beliefs and really in contrast of what I wanted for them in the first place because they believe they are a failure in my eyes.

I am a teacher by personality, I'm an engineer by education; God has given me spiritual strengths in exhortation–I understand paths and solutions.

My Life's Motto: I'm here to help you! Requested or not.

I don't know about you, but when my children, and Jean, my wife, mention an area they are struggling with and I jump in with steps 1–2- 4 & 8 to "fix" the problem instead of listening to them and just agreeing there is a legitimate struggle, they quit coming to me at all, and I have to find out by some other way that there is a problem and then try to be invited into their life to help.

"I don't have it together" kids do not feel comfortable sharing their struggles with "have it all together" parents because they don't

feel the parents understand their struggle. They will attempt to fix the situation on their own, sometimes with the help of their friends, and then come to you with the problem already solved seeking your approval.

I love what John Eldridge says in his Wild at Heart materials, "Our wives (and I add in our children), are not a problem to be solved, they are a mystery to be understood."

(And all of the people said, "AMEN!")

You don't have to air all of your dirty laundry and every impure thought you've ever had with your children; you know that is not what I am saying. But they must see realness in you. Fleshing it out as you fail and fall and trust and try again, because you do, and I do. That is life. Scripture says we "work out our salvation with fear and trembling". It doesn't say we walk through the tulips with flute and tambourine. Be real, especially with your older kids and let them see God as the one who gets you through and maybe they will trust *Him* to get them through—instead of you!

Now one other thing, as a result of some of the places these materials will take them. Your kids, however young or older will very possibly have shared or wish to share some very deep parts of their hearts about their struggles and stumbles in this area of relationships and physical intimacy with someone who will listen and be supportive in their life. Now as I just said that, some of you are already aware of the risk of being "embarrassed" by your kiddos. Be careful here because *pride* will make you more concerned about being embarrassed by what your young person might say and share or what they might actually admit doing, than you are rejoicing over their brokenness of heart and desire for a restored purity in their life and in their relationship with their Heavenly Father.

Shame on us, for I too have responded in the same way–fearful of looking bad and being embarrassed.

The rest of you will disguise your pride by smugly thinking, "My kids would never have done anything like that!"

We are wrong–every kid, *every kid*–including your parent's children and my parents' children, you and I, have done in our minds and hearts and many of us with our bodies every imaginable act seeking for validation and acceptance.

Isaiah 53:6, "We all, like sheep, have gone astray,
each of us has turned to his own way;
and the LORD has laid on him the iniquity of us all."

If you are like me, your next response might be, "Well why didn't they come to us rather than open up at some dumpy retreat or to their youth pastor or whomever?" Can it be very likely they know from experience how we will respond?

Don't miss this next thought. "If being vulnerable and honest with their struggles gets them the same responses and results as getting caught–why risk it. Why not just wait and see if they get caught?"

Hear that again. *If being vulnerable and honest with their struggles gets them the same response and results as getting caught–why risk it?*

Now, Dads and Moms, one big word of encouragement, when you thought you had established a better relationship with your kids than they are showing right now and you wonder if they ever listen to what you say anymore–they do! They may not acknowledge it or respond to it–but they hear it. Because truth is truth, and if it is wrapped in love, it has an almost uncanny way of finding a crevice to fit into and grow, even in the toughest rocks. "*...so is my word that goes out from my* *mouth: It will not return to me empty...,* " (Isaiah 55:11) doesn't just apply to quoting scripture. Truth is truth, and if it is truth, it originated with God and always accomplishes its purposes.

Thank you for the pleasure of your company on this journey of the heart. I pray it has been more than you hoped and that it lives out better than you could have dreamed!

jh

Zephaniah 3:17